The COOKBOOK for PEOPLE WHO LOVE ANIMALS

Gentle World

Introduction by Michael A. Klaper, M.D.

This book is dedicated to the animals, with the hope that it will help to alleviate and eventually eliminate their unfathomable suffering.

Special thanks to Jay and Freya Dinshah, without whose help this cookbook would probably still be in manuscript form.

100% recycled paper.

Eighth Edition

ISBN 0-929274-18-0
Library of Congress Catalog Card No. 87-082778

Gentle World Publishing.
P.O Box 238
Kapa'au
Hawai'i 96755

e-mail: gentle@aloha.net

website: www.gentleworld.org

Contents

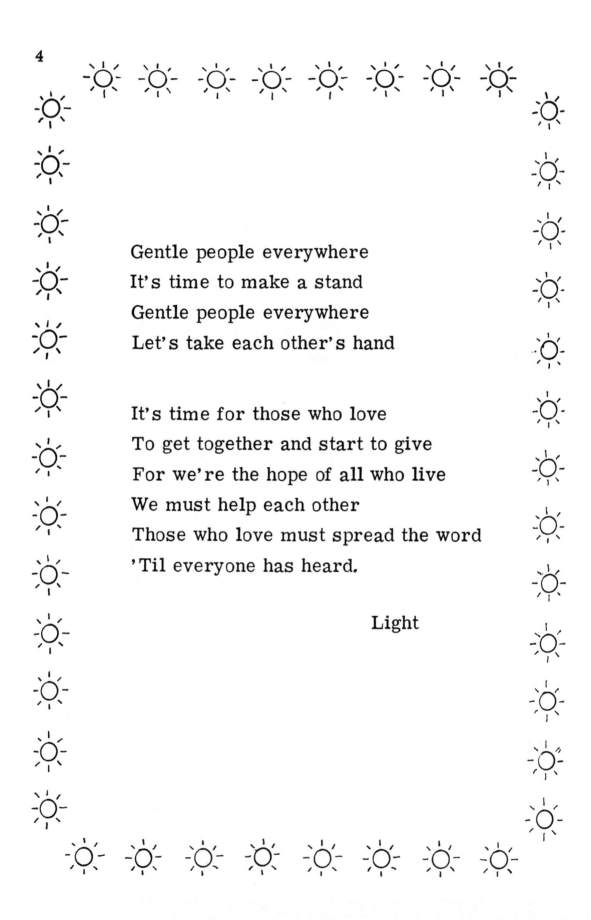

Gentle people everywhere
It's time to make a stand
Gentle people everywhere
Let's take each other's hand

It's time for those who love
To get together and start to give
For we're the hope of all who live
We must help each other
Those who love must spread the word
'Til everyone has heard.

Light

INTRODUCTION

To be alive in this decade is an adventure and a challenge. These are times of great change and of powerful forces at work. Although problems such as overpopulation, pollution, war, and world hunger may seem overwhelming, there is also great reason for hope. New understandings are dawning in minds and hearts of people around the world.

Public health studies in America have revealed that the epidemics of heart disease and cancers have been conclusively linked to unhealthful diet. The high fat, high protein, low fiber diet consumed by most Americans, clogs the human system as surely as using kerosene for fuel could ruin the engine of your car. It is now clear that the human body becomes lean, strong and healthy when run on a "fuel" free of the fat of animals and rich in the grains, legumes, fruits, and vegetables that the earth provides so generously. Such a diet has always been the natural human diet, but now it offers itself as a key for our survival as individuals and as a species.

THE COOKBOOK FOR PEOPLE WHO LOVE ANIMALS is more than a collection of recipes for delicious, healthful food. It is a gateway to spiritual growth as well as physical health. Non-violence in obtaining food is the world's next step in development. The preparation and enjoyment of this food does not cause suffering to any feeling creature. With the simple act of ceasing to eat animals, the body not only becomes healthier, but the entire planet becomes a saner, gentler home for ALL its inhabitants. Improved health is the deserved reward for those who eat a harmless diet.

The suggested meal plans will guide you through your day's eating, with foods that are fully nutritionally balanced and satisfying to your palate. The hearty meals of pastas, vegetable loaves, "superburgers", and many more, supply ample protein yet do not rob the bones of their calcium as concentrated meat-protein does.

Enjoy this food. It is the RIGHT food for human beings. Your body will thank you for your wisdom, and the animals for your compassion.

Michael A. Klaper, M.D.

NUTRITIONAL ASSURANCE

Not only are the colors, aromas and flavors of vegan cuisine a delight for the senses, but how animal-free food meets your body's nutritional needs borders on a panacea. Rest assured that ALL your requirements for protein, carbohydrates, vitamins, minerals, and fiber are fully supplied by the wide variety of grains, legumes, vegetables, seeds, and fruits used in vegan cookery.

THE RIGHT FUEL FOR THE "BODY ENGINE"

Our cells, those building blocks of our body, are made to run on carbohydrates—the sugars and starches from plants. Carbohydrates are burned for energy, unlike animal fat which is stored under our skin. Calories from animal fat tend to "stick" to you, while those from carbohydrates do not. You needn't worry about "gaining weight on all that starch" in potatoes, whole grain breads, and pastas IF you are not also eating animal fats in meat and dairy products.

MEAT-EATING AMERICANS EAT TOO MUCH PROTEIN. Eating meat floods the body with protein waste products. The kidneys must "flush" these wastes into the urine and calcium is used to do this. This continuing urinary loss of calcium eventually robs calcium from the bones, leading to osteoporosis ("thin bones"). Vegetable protein, especially in whole grain, fiber-rich form, is "safer" protein, less concentrated, and absorbed slowly into the bloodstream. The small amount that we need each day (20-40 grams, or about the weight of ten pennies) is amply supplied by the protein-rich foods listed on page 188. As for meeting your vitamin and mineral needs, these are found in abundance in green and yellow vegetables (also see charts, pages 187, 188).

Try not to overcook any food. Avoid using refined carbohydrates like white sugar and white flour, and try not to mix fruits and vegetables at the same meal. It is also advisable to delay drinking water for at least thirty minutes after a meal to avoid diluting the digestive juices. Take time to enjoy the chewing and tasting of this wonderful food.

Michael A. Klaper, M.D.

Dr. Klaper is a graduate of the University Of Illinois College Of Medicine, with postgraduate training and experience in surgery, anesthesia, and obstetrics, and in general practice since 1973. He presently lectures nationwide and practices nutritional counseling in central Florida.

PREPARING TO COOK

Vegan cuisine can be prepared in any kitchen with standard kitchen utensils. Here is a list of cooking accessories that prove to be especially useful and that you may want to acquire:

UTENSILS

Stainless Steel Pots and Pans
 (Avoid aluminum cookware)

Cast Iron or Porcelain Pots and Pans

Vegetable Steamer

Pyrex and Corningware Baking
 Casseroles

Wooden Bowls and Spoons

Blender

Vegetable Scrub Brush

Mortar and Pestle

Pressure Cooker

Wok

CHAMPION JUICER—An electrical appliance that juices, homogenizes, and grates. Makes fruit juices, nut butters, ice cream from frozen bananas, and grates vegetables.

FOOD MILL—A hand held device for making sauces (apple, pear, tomato, etc.). It creates a smooth sauce consistency while screening out pits and skins.

NUT GRINDER—A small electrical appliance for grinding up nuts and seeds.

FOOD PROCESSOR—A powerful electrical appliance that slices, grates and blends. Good for making coleslaw, tofu yogurt, etc.

NOTE: In baking cookies, muffins, and bread, the temperature will vary according to the accuracy of the individual oven. A safe guideline is 350 F.

Glossary Of Ingredients

ARROWROOT POWDER— Thickener, used in place of corn starch or flour to thicken gravies, soups, cooked fruits and jams, carob pudding, and vegetable sautés. (Gives the sauté a Chinese flavor and consistency.) Always sprinkle into food through a fine strainer, stir in well, and allow to cook.

BEAN THREADS— Clear, spaghetti-type Chinese noodles made from mung bean sprouts. Easy to prepare.

CAROB ("St. John's Bread")— A cocoa-like powder (from locust-tree pods) used in place of chocolate. Low in fat, and having a naturally sweet flavor, it is usually available and used in the toasted form.

DATE SUGAR— Used as a sweetener, made from dried dates. It is best used in addition to a liquid sweetener such as sorghum. Can be used in any recipe that calls for sweetener.

DATE SYRUP— Dark colored, heavy syrup used as a sweetener. Also made from dried dates. Excellent in baking cookies and cakes.

GINGER ROOT— A seasoning, especially good in Chinese dishes. Always peel it, dice it and use sparingly as it is very strong. It is also good as a breath freshener.

GRAINS AND WHOLE-GRAIN PRODUCTS— Brown rice, barley, millet, corn, oats, cous-cous, buckwheat groats (kasha), bulghur wheat, and products made from them; i.e., cereals, flour, pastas, breads, etc.

GREEN VEGETABLES— Sources of protein, vitamins, and minerals. Get to know and love them: Collards, broccoli, Brussels sprouts, cabbage, kale, dark lettuce, mustard greens, spinach, Swiss chard, endive, zucchini, asparagus, etc.

KELP— A powdered form of seaweed. It is rich in iodine; has a slightly salty taste. Good on salads, in salad dressings, and on avocados. Used mostly on raw foods. At our table, it has replaced salt.

LEGUMES— Protein bonanzas! Anything that grows in a pod. Of best use to the body when eaten with whole grains: $2\frac{1}{2}$ parts grains to 1 part legumes. Beans of all types (kidney, pinto, navy, lima, soy, aduki, etc.), lentils, chick peas (garbanzos), etc. Use in soups, stews, tacos, chili, casseroles, mash into sandwich spreads, etc.

MAPLE SYRUP— Amber liquid sweetener, the boiled sap of sugar-maple trees. Good source of calcium and magnesium; excellent in baking and cooking. Also comes in granules (maple sugar).

MILLET— A grain, known as the Queen of grains; the richest source of protein of all grains. Great served plain or in casseroles and burgers.

NUTRITIONAL YEAST— Pleasant golden powder or flakes. Rich in protein and B-vitamins, it has a delicious cheesy taste. Great on salads, in soups, and sprinkled on casseroles. It can be made into a gravy or a cheese sauce.

OILS— We use only cold-pressed vegetable oils. A good oil is necessary in cooking, baking, and dressings. Good ones are safflower, sunflower, sesame, soy, and olive.

OKARA— A by-product of making tofu. It is soy pulp (good in salads, as a base in burgers, excellent for animals).

POSTUM— Made from bran, wheat, and molasses. Used as a coffee substitute.

SEA SALT— Salt crystallized from sea water: contains iodine, manganese, and other trace minerals.

SEA VEGETABLES— Kelp, dulse, nori, kombu, arame, etc., contain vitamin B12, iodine, manganese, selenium, calcium, and other minerals. Good on salads and in dressings. Kelp can be used in a shaker to replace salt on the table.

SEEDS— High in protein and essential oils. Can be mixed in blender with cold water and a dash of sweetener to make a "milk" for pouring over cereal, used in baking, etc. Sunflower, sesame, and pumpkin seeds should be purchased raw for eating or cooking, or can be roasted in the oven for toppings and treats.

SORGHUM— A sweetener in thick syrup form, extracted from pure sorghum wheat juice. Can be used as a sweetener in any recipe.

SOY POWDER— Made from cooked soy beans, it contains all the natural oil of the soy bean. Used in casseroles, sweets, and for making soy milk. It can also be used as an EGG SUBSTITUTE: Use 1 heaping tablespoon soy powder and 2 tablespoons of water, in place of 1 egg.

SPROUTS— High in protein and vitamins. Easy to make yourself, or to buy fresh at the supermarket. Use alfalfa, lentils, mung beans, sunflower seeds, wheatberries, etc.

SWEETENERS— Sorghum, maple syrup, barley malt syrup, rice syrup (yinny), natural fruit juices, date sugar or blenderized dates, puréed fruits. Use them to replace honey or sugar, on cereal, in baking and other recipes, etc.

STOCK— As used in this cookbook: Water in which vegetables have been cooked; this liquid is then used as a base for soups, gravies, or sauces.

TAHINI— Tahini is a "butter" made from ground, unsalted sesame seeds (a rich source of protein, calcium, and phosphorus), used in many ways in vegan cuisine: as a foundation for sauces and salad dressings, a "binder" or egg substitute for casseroles and burgers, a topping for fruit, a spread on bread.

TAMARI— Classic soy sauce, made from soy beans, water, wheat, and sea salt, aged and fermented. A very tasty seasoning, but use sparingly, due to its sodium content.

TOFU— A mild soy-cheese, rich in protein and calcium. Extemely versatile, can be substituted for meat, eggs, milk, and cheese (see recipes). Can be used to make: scrambled tofu, "yogurt", "cream cheese", "mayonnaise", "cream pies", puddings, lasagna, etc.

TVP (Textured Vegetable Protein)— Granules made from soy beans. Prepare by adding hot water; adds a hearty texture to spaghetti sauce, chili, soups, casseroles, burgers, etc.

VANILLA— Where vanilla is mentioned, it is the commercial liquid extract. The solvent of this is alcohol, which evaporates upon heating, leaving the vanilla flavor in the food. In uncooked recipes, such as certain desserts, the solvent would remain in the food. In such cases, it may be omitted; or, you can make a water-extract: Slit a vanilla bean down the length of one side, let stand in water (or sesame, soy, or nut milk) for 2 hours or more (less if liquid is warm). After soaking, remove bean, dry and store for future re-use. Use the flavored liquid in place of other liquid in recipe. Most of the flavor comes from the seeds; so, after soaking for the last time, the seeds can be scraped out of the pod and also used for flavoring.

YELLOW VEGETABLES— Good for key vitamins. Have some every day or two in salads, vegetable bakes, steamed in side dishes, soups, etc. Learn to appreciate corn, sweet potatoes, squash (summer, butternut, Hubbard, spaghetti, acorn), parsnips, rutabaga, popcorn, etc.

DAIRY PRODUCTS—WHO NEEDS THEM?

Dairy products laden with butterfat and concentrated protein (casein) contribute to clogged arteries, and allergic/inflammatory reactions such as chronic runny noses, recurrent ear and bronchial infections, asthmatic bronchitis, and other inflammations of joints, skin (eczema), and bowels (colitis).

No other animal drinks mother's milk after weaning, certainly not the milk from another species. Cow's milk is not a natural food for man, woman or child and should be eliminated from the diet as well as products made from it: cheese, ice cream, yogurt, butter, sour cream, sherbet, etc. Millions live healthily without dairy products, and so should you.

We are told to eat dairy products because they are good sources of calcium and protein. Actually, they are a wholesome source of neither. The calcium is accompanied by a large load of phosphate and protein that can neutralize the good effects of the calcium and actually contribute to osteoporosis ("thin bones"). Milk protein is very dissimilar from human protein and can cause the allergic/inflammatory reactions listed above. The butterfat in milk is a dangerous artery-clogging contributor to heart disease. Realize the huge butterfat content of these dairy favorites: whole milk, 3%; ice cream, 25%; cheese, 20-25%; milk chocolate, 25-28%.

So what are good sources of calcium and protein? On a meatless diet, your body needs only 400-1000 milligrams of calcium daily, easily obtainable in green vegetables, nuts and seeds. A serving of cooked collards or broccoli has as much USABLE calcium as a glass of milk. Almonds and raisins, tofu dishes, tahini (sesame) dressing and more meet most people's calcium needs. If there is a need for extra calcium, have extra helpings of calcium-rich foods. Ample protein is available from the grains, legumes, green vegetables, nuts and seeds listed on page 187.

The recipes for tasty alternatives to dairy fat products are in the "Breakfast" and "Treats" sections; you'll be surprised at how sunflower, almond, or other nut milks made quickly in your blender resemble the taste of dairy milk on your cereal. For treats, "Tofu Yogurt" or "Tahini Banana Malted" are easy delights.

Be wary of dairy:

1. Skim milk offers little advantage over whole milk—it still has 1/3 the butterfat of whole milk (you don't need any) and a full complement of allergy-inciting milk protein.

2. For daily drinking instead of milk, drink liquids such as pure water, nut and seed milks, fruit and vegetable juices, herbal teas, and caffeine-free coffee substitutes, etc.

3. Milk and dairy products are hidden in many commercial products such as breads, baked goods, candy, etc. Skim milk powder is a frequent ingredient and is often listed as "casein", or "sodium caseinate", the chemical name for milk protein. This is still milk powder, just as prone to cause allergic reactions. A by-product of the cheese-making process called "whey" is also used frequently. Become a reader of labels, and if you see "whey powder" or "casein", pass it by.

Without dairy fat in your blood, you can become leaner and healthier, and reduce your chances of heart attack, stroke, and various forms of cancer. So who needs dairy? In my professional opinion, only the calves.

Michael A. Klaper, M.D.

Breakfast Recipes

BANANA MILK
Yields 2 cups

1 banana   1 teaspoon sorghum (optional)
1/2 frozen banana   1 teaspoon vanilla (optional)
1/2 to 1 cup water

Slice the bananas and place in a blender. Add 1/2 cup water, sorghum and vanilla. Add additional water gradually to reach desired consistency (either thick or thin is good).
  Drink as is, or pour over granola, other cereals, or fruit.

VARIATION

Add 1 teaspoon carob powder with the water, for chocolate banana milk.

NUT MILK
Yields 1 to 1-1/2 cups

1/4 cup nut butter   1 cup water

Put ingredients in blender. Blend at high speed for 30 seconds.
  This makes regular nut milk.

OR:

1/4 cup nut butter   3/4 cup water

Blend at high speed for 30 seconds.
  This makes thick nut milk.

VARIATION

Use a variety of nut and seed butters: peanut butter, cashew butter, almond butter, sesame tahini butter, sunflower seed butter. Add 1 teaspoon of vanilla to mixture while blending.

QUICK INSTANT SOY MILK
Yields 2 cups

2 cups water   8 tablespoons soy powder

Place all the ingredients in a blender and blend for 30 seconds at medium speed. For a thicker milk, add 2 more tablespoons soy powder.

SOY MILK
Yields 4 quarts

2 cups soybeans   6 cups soaking water
Approximately 8 cups water for blending

Soak 2 cups soybeans overnight in 6 cups water. Then pour off the water and place 1 cup soybeans and 2-1/3 cups water in a blender and blend at high speed for 1 minute. Transfer bean mixture to a large pot. Repeat process with remaining beans. Cover loosely and cook over low heat until it boils, reduce heat as low as possible and cook for 45 minutes longer. Do not cook with a tight cover or the mixture will boil over. When finished cooking, cool and strain the mixture through cheesecloth, to obtain a liquid soymilk and a pulp. Store both in the refrigerator.

The soymilk, as a beverage, can be used plain, or if desired, sweetened to taste with 1 tablespoon sorghum, or 1 teaspoon vanilla, or 1/2 banana blended into the milk before serving.

Soymilk can also be used for making mayonnaise or tofu. The pulp can be used in cooking: grains, casseroles, burgers, dog food, etc.

TOFU YOGURT
Yields 2 cups

1 12-ounce cake tofu   1-2 tablespoons sweetener
1 banana, frozen and sliced   1/4 cup fruit juice or water
1 ripe banana, sliced   1 teaspoon vanilla (optional)

Combine all the ingredients in a blender; blend at medium speed for 45 seconds, until creamy. To serve, add fruit, raisins, and sunflower seeds.

If you use a food processor, you can omit the liquid, then the yogurt will be thicker and creamier.

VARIATION

After yogurt is made, blend with strawberries, blueberries, cherries, peaches, or any fresh fruit. Chill in freezer for 30 minutes.

SOY MARGARINE
Yields 1 cup

1/2 cup soy powder   1 tablespoon sweetener (sorghum)
1/4 cup water   1/4 teaspoon sea salt
1/4 cup oil

In a small bowl, combine the soy powder and the water. Add the oil, sorghum, and salt. Chill and serve.

VARIATION

Combine all ingredients in a blender instead of a bowl. Add a ripe banana and 1/4 teaspoon vanilla. Serve as is, or freeze overnight. Defrost for 10 minutes before serving.

SOY TOFU
Yields 3 8-ounce cakes

2 quarts soymilk   3 lemons
(See recipe)

Combine warm soymilk with the juice of 3 lemons; stir gently 3 times. Cover and allow to sit for 15 minutes until the milk curdles. Ladle the milk into a collander lined with a piece of cheesecloth. Fold the cloth over the curd and place a 2 to 3 pound weight on top; allow the curd to drain and solidify for 30 minutes. Store tofu in container and cover with cold water. Keep refrigerated.

SCRAMBLED TOFU
Serves 2

1 tablespoon oil   4 tablespoons nutritional yeast
2 8-ounce cakes tofu   1/2 teaspoon kelp
1/2 teaspoon sea salt   1/8 teaspoon turmeric

Heat the oil in a skillet over medium-high heat. Crumble the tofu by hand and drop into the hot skillet, flipping constantly with a spatula. Season with the salt, nutritional yeast, kelp, and turmeric. Cook for 5 to 7 minutes, until tofu starts to brown. Serve like eggs for breakfast or any meal.

VARIATION

In oiled skillet, lightly saute a sliced onion, until transparent, and diced green pepper, if desired, before adding the tofu and proceeding as above.

TOFU COTTAGE CHEESE
Serves 4

1 8-ounce cake tofu   1/2 teaspoon dill weed
1 tablespoon oil   1 teaspoon tamari
1 teaspoon vinegar   1 teaspoon nutritional yeast
or, 1 teaspoon lemon juice

Mash the tofu cake. Add the remaining ingredients and mix well. Chill and serve.

TOFU CREAM CHEESE
Serves 4

1 12-ounce cake tofu
1/8 to 1/2 teaspoon sea salt
1/8 teaspoon caraway seeds

1/4 teaspoon dill weed or seed
Juice of 3 small limes
2 tablespoons water

Place all the ingredients in a blender. Blend until creamy. Serve for breakfast on bread, pancakes, or with baked potatoes.

STRAWBERRY JAM
Yields 4 cups

3 to 4 cups strawberries
1/4 cup water

1/4 cup sorghum
2 to 3 teaspoons arrowroot powder

Place the strawberries in a large pot with the water; cook over low heat for 20 minutes. Add the sorghum; sift the arrowroot in, stirring constantly. Cook for approximately 20 minutes, until very soft. Add additional sweetening to taste.

VARIATION

Substitute peaches, apples, or grapes for the strawberries.

BLUEBERRY JAM
Yields 4 cups

3 cups blueberries
1/4 cup water
1/2 teaspoon vanilla (optional)
2 to 3 teaspoons arrowroot powder

1/4 cup sorghum or date sugar
or 1/8 cup sorghum and
1/8 cup date sugar

Put the blueberries and water in a medium sized pot, and place over low heat, being careful not to burn the berries. The juice will be released after several minutes; watch that it doesn't boil over. Add the sorghum and the vanilla.

Slowly sift the arrowroot in for thickness, stirring constantly. Cook for approximately 20 minutes, until thick and creamy. For smoother texture, blend for 30 seconds. Chill and serve.

PEACH WHIP
Yields 1 cup

5 to 7 peaches   1 tablespoon soy powder (optional)
2 tablespoons sorghum (optional)

Peel the peaches, slice into a blender and blend 1 minute at medium speed.
Add the sweetener and soy powder, if desired.
Or: Cook the peaches in a large pot for 30 minutes until soft. Place in a
blender and blend for a few seconds at medium speed.

VARIATION

Substitute any fruit for the peaches. Serve for breakfast over muffins, with
cereal, with seeds and raisins, or on bread.

ALMOND-RAISIN WHIP
Yields 1 cup

1/2 cup raw almonds   1/2 teaspoon vanilla
1/2 cup water   1/2 cup raisins
2 tablespoons soy powder

Soak the almonds in water to cover overnight. Drain the almonds, reserving
1/2 cup of the liquid. Place all the ingredients and the reserved liquid in a
blender and blend until creamy and smooth. To thin, add several drops of
water or orange juice.

PLUM WHIP
Yields 3 cups

2 pounds plums, pitted (any type)   1/2 teaspoon vanilla (optional)
1/4 cup water   2 tablespoons soy powder
1/3 cup sweetener

Cut the plums into bite size pieces. Combine with the water in a saucepan and
cook over low heat for 30 minutes until soft. Remove from heat; add the
sweetener, and vanilla if desired. Transfer to blender; add the soy powder
and whip for 30 seconds. Serve on bread, muffins, in cereal, or as a filling
for pastry.

VARIATION

Substitute peaches, cherries, nectarines, or other fruit for the plums.

APPLE BUTTER
Yields 4 cups

15 to 20 apples, peeled and cored   2-1/2 teaspoons cinnamon
1/2 cup water   2-1/2 tablespoons sorghum

Cut the apples into chunks and place in a large pot. Add the water and cook over a low heat (for approximately 1 hour), stirring often. Add the cinnamon and sorghum; cook for approximately 1 hour more. The sauce will become darker and thicker the longer it is cooked. Add a little more cinnamon and sorghum. Cook with lid off, stirring often, for 30 minutes, until smooth and thick.

UNCOOKED APPLE SAUCE
Serves 4

6 to 10 apples, peeled and cored   1 tablespoon sorghum
1 to 1-1/2 cups water   (optional if apples are not sweet)

Cut the apples into bite size pieces. Place a handful of apples with 2 ounces of water in a blender and blend until smooth. Continue this process until all the apples are blended. Sweeten before serving if desired.

VARIATION

Substitute peaches, pears, or other fruits for the apples. Add raisins while blending.

EASY APPLE SAUCE
Serves 7

15 to 20 apples, peeled and cored   1 teaspoon cinnamon
1/2 cup water   1 tablespoon sorghum

Cut the apples into chunks and place in a large pot. Add the water, cover and simmer over a low heat, stirring often, until the apples become soft, for approximately 30 minutes. Add the cinnamon and sorghum. Cook until creamy and soft. Blend to use for a creamy sauce, or mash.

VARIATION

Substitute peaches, nectarines, pears etc., or any combination of a few fruits for the apples.

SOAKED RAISINS

1 cup raisins   1/2 cup orange juice or water

Wash raisins well. Place in a container with the liquid and cover. Allow to sit over night in refrigerator. Delicious for breakfast.

VARIATION

Substitute dates, figs, or other dried fruit in place of the raisins. Also try different fruit juices for the liquid.

STEWED PRUNES
Yields 1 pound

1 pound of prunes, pitted   1 cinnamon stick
3 cups water

Combine all the ingredients in a medium saucepan. Cover and simmer over low heat for approximately 20 minutes. Serve warm or cold.

VARIATION

Add 1/2 cup raisins before cooking

COMPOTE–FRUIT SOUP
Serves 7

5 plums (any kind)   1 cup grapes
2 pears   2 nectarines
5 peaches   1/4 cup water
2 apples   1/4 cup sorghum (optional)
1 cup cherries

Pit all of the fruit, peeling any rough skins, and cut into bite size pieces. Place in a medium size pot; add the water. Cover and cook over medium heat for approximately 14 minutes, or until the fruit is soft. Add sweetener to taste. Do not allow the compote to become a mush. Allow to cool; store in a glass container. The compote can be frozen for later use.

FRUIT SALAD
Serves 4

5 pounds mixed red and yellow   1/4 cup raisins
   sweet apples, peeled and sliced   3 tablespoons sunflower seeds
2 bananas, sliced   1/2 cup coconut, grated
2 navel oranges, peeled and divided 1/2 cup orange juice (optional)

Arrange the apple slices in a large bowl. Add banana and orange slices, raisins, and sunflower seeds. Top with coconut. Serve with orange juice topping if desired.

SUN GRANOLA
Yields 2 cookie sheets

4 cups rolled oats
1/2 cup wheat germ or bran
   or 1/4 cup wheat germ and
   1/4 cup bran
1 cup sunflower seeds
1 cup crushed walnuts, cashews,
   peanuts, or a mixture
2/3 cup flour

1 teaspoon cinnamon
1/2 cup oil
1 cup sorghum
1 teaspoon vanilla
1/4 teaspoon sea salt
1/8 cup water
1/2 cup corn meal (optional)

Preheat oven to 275 F. In a large bowl, combine all the liquid ingredients. In a separate bowl, combine all the dry ingredients. Add the dry ingredients to the liquid and mix well. Place mixture on 2 cookie sheets, spread out evenly. Bake for 20 minutes; turn over and bake for 20 minutes more.

VARIATION

Add 1/2 cup sesame seeds or 1/2 cup shredded coconut to the dry ingredients.

OATMEAL CRUNCH
Serves 4

2 cups rolled oats
1/2 cup sunflower seeds
1 teaspoon cinnamon
1/2 cup chopped cashews

1/3 cup oil
1/2 cup sweetener, sorghum
1/4 cup water or apple juice
1 teaspoon vanilla

Preheat oven to 275 F. Combine the dry ingredients in a bowl. In a separate bowl, combine the wet ingredients. Add the dry ingredients to wet ingredients, and mix well. Spread out evenly on a cookie sheet. Bake for approximately 45 minutes, or until almost dry. Remove with spatula.
   Serve warm or store in canisters.

WHEAT GERM CEREAL WITH BANANA MILK
Serves 1

1/2 cup wheat germ
1/4 cup bran
1 teaspoon sunflower seeds

1/3 cup raisins
2 cups banana milk, (see recipe)

Combine the wheat germ and bran in a large cereal bowl. Add the sunflower seeds and raisins. Pour the banana milk over this mixture and serve.

HOT CEREAL
Serves 5 to 6

5 cups water	3 to 4 tablespoons sorghum
2 cups rolled oats	1 teaspoon margarine
1/2 teaspoon vanilla (optional)	(vegetable, non-chemical)
1/4 teaspoon cinnamon (optional)	1/4 teaspoon sea salt

Combine the water and oats in a medium saucepan. Cook covered over medium heat for approximately 5 minutes or until bubbling. Reduce heat; and simmer uncovered, for 15 minutes or until the oats are soft, stirring occasionally. Add the vanilla, sorghum, cinnamon, and margarine. For a creamier cereal, simmer for 5 minutes longer.

VARIATION

Substitute or combine the oats with other grains such as: rye flakes, wheat flakes, or millet. The basic measurements stay the same, but these grains take longer to cook (approximately 30 minutes). Add other grains before the oats. Add one sliced banana, 1/2 cup of raisins, or 1/2 cup fruit juice, during the last few minutes of cooking.

FRIED PLANTAIN
Serves 3 to 4

2 or 3 large, ripe plantain	4 tablespoons vegetable oil

Cut the plantain into 1/4-inch thick slices, lengthwise or crosswise. Heat the vegetable oil. Place in a medium size frying pan over medium-high heat. Add the plantain slices and fry until browned on both sides. Serve plain or with syrup.

PLANTAIN SOUFFLE
Serves 4 to 6

1/8 cup water	2 tablespoons sorghum
3 ripe plantain, sliced	1 teaspoon baking soda
2 ripe bananas, sliced	1/2 teaspoon cinnamon

Preheat oven to 375 F. In a blender, blend small amounts at a time, at high speed, until all the ingredients are blended together.
Place in a medium sized casserole bowl. Bake for 30 to 45 minutes.

BAKED PLANTAIN
Serves 1 or 2

1 ripe plantain

Preheat oven to 350 F. Bake the plantain for 30 minutes unpeeled, until the skin is black and the plantain is tender. Peel and slice to serve. Serve at breakfast.
Tastes great!

PLANTAIN PATTIES
Serves 3 to 5

2 ripe plantain
1 banana
1/2 frozen banana (optional)
1/4 teaspoon cinnamon

1/2 teaspoon sorghum
1/4 cup water or orange juice
1 tablespoon oil

Preheat oven to 350 F. Blend all the ingredients, except the oil, in a blender for 30 seconds at medium speed. Oil a cookie sheet. Using a tablespoon, drop the plantain mixture onto the cookie sheet. Bake for 7 minutes, or until golden brown; flip the patties over, and bake for 3 minutes longer.
    Or, heat the oil in a large skillet, over medium-high heat; add teaspoonfuls of the batter, and fry the patties on both sides until golden brown.
    Serve with jam.

QUICK BUCKWHEAT PANCAKES
Serves 4

1 cup buckwheat flour
3/4 cup whole wheat pastry flour
3/4 teaspoon baking soda
2 tablespoons soy powder

4 tablespoons water
2 tablespoons sorghum
1/3 cup oil
1-2/3 cup soy or nut milk
    (see recipe)

Combine the flours and soda in a medium-sized mixing bowl. Mix the soy powder, water and sorghum together in a large bowl. Add the oil and milk. Add the dry ingredients and stir a few times to form a thick batter. Oil a griddle and place over medium-high heat. Pour the batter onto the griddle forming small circles. Cook for approximately 3 minutes on each side, or until golden brown.

NUTRITIONAL YEAST PANCAKES
Yields 2 dozen

1/2 cup nutritional yeast
1 cup whole wheat flour

1 cup water
1 tablespoon vegetable oil

Combine the yeast, flour, and water in a medium sized bowl, to form a loose flakey mixture. Heat the oil in a large skillet over medium-high heat. Pour the batter into the skillet, forming small circles. Cook for approximately 3 minutes on each side, until golden brown and crispy.

VARIATION

Add small pieces of tofu or strawberries, blueberries or raisins to the batter before cooking.

APPLE CARROT MUFFINS
Yields 1 dozen

2-1/2 cups whole wheat flour
1/2 cup soy powder
1 teaspoon baking soda
1/2 teaspoon sea salt
1/2 teaspoon nutmeg
1/2 teaspoon cinnamon

2/3 cup oil
3/4 cup sorghum
1 teaspoon vanilla
1/2 cup apple, grated
1/2 cup carrot, grated

Preheat oven to 400 F. In a medium sized bowl, combine all the dry ingredients. Combine all the liquid ingredients in a large bowl; stir in the apple and carrot. Add the dry ingredients to the liquid mixture, Oil one muffin tin: spoon the batter into the cups until 2/3 full. Bake for 20 minutes, or until a toothpick stuck in the center of the muffin, comes out dry.

BRAN MUFFINS
Yields 1 dozen

1-1/4 cups whole wheat flour
1 cup bran
1 teaspoon baking soda
1 teaspoon cinnamon

1/3 cup oil
1/3 to 1/2 cup sorghum
1 cup soymilk (see recipe)
1 teaspoon vanilla

Preheat oven to 400 F. Combine all the dry ingredients in a large bowl. Mix all liquid ingredients in a large bowl; add the dry ingredients and mix well. Oil one muffin tin; sprinkle each cup with flour. Spoon batter into each cup until half full. Bake for 25 minutes.

VARIATION

Add raisins or blueberries, grated apple or grated carrots to the batter before baking.

WHOLE WHEAT BAGELS
Yields 2-1/2 dozen

2 tablespoons baking yeast
6 tablespoons date sugar
2 cups warm water
2 cups whole wheat pastry flour

1/2 cup oil
2 teaspoons salt
4 cups whole wheat pastry flour
 (additional)
3 quarts of water

In a large bowl, combine yeast, date sugar, and warm water. Slowly add 2 cups flour. Mix well, let rise, 10 minutes. Beat in oil, salt and about 4 more cups flour. Mix well. Turn dough onto a floured board, knead for 10 minutes. The dough should be soft but not sticky. Place the dough in an oiled bowl; cover with a clean dishcloth and allow to rise 45 minutes. Turn onto a floured board and knead for 10 minutes more. Cut pieces of dough and roll into ropes approximately 7" long and 1 inch round. Join the ends to form a doughnut shape. Let rise 5 minutes.

Preheat oven to 375 F. Bring the 3 quarts of water to a boil, in a large soup pot. Drop 4 or 5 of the rings, 1 at a time (risen side down), into the boiling water, and put lid on. Boil for 30 seconds on 1 side, then 30 seconds on the other, keeping a rapid boil all the time. Remove bagels with slotted spatula and place about 1/2-inch apart on a well-oiled cookie sheet. Bake for 25 to 30 minutes or until golden brown.

CARAWAY PUFFINS
Yields 1 dozen

1-1/3 cups whole wheat flour
1 tablespoon dry active yeast
2 teaspoons caraway seeds
1 cup thick soymilk (see recipe)
1/4 cup water

2 tablespoons sorghum
1 tablespoon oil
1 teaspoon sea salt
3 teaspoons chopped onions
1 cup whole wheat pastry flour

In a large bowl, combine the flour, yeast and caraway seeds. In a blender, combine the soymilk, water, sorghum, oil, salt and onion; blend at medium speed for one minute until smooth. Add to the dry ingredients; mix with electric mixer for 3 minutes at high speed. Stir in the pastry flour. Place dough in an oiled bowl, cover and allow to rise for 1-1/2 hours. Oil a muffin tin. Divide the dough into 12 equal parts. Fill each muffin cup halfway with batter. Cover and allow to rise for 30 to 45 minutes until doubled in bulk.

Preheat oven to 400 F. Bake the muffins for 12 to 15 minutes. Serve hot.

CORN MUFFINS
Yields 1 dozen

1 cup sorghum
1-1/4 cup thick soymilk (see recipe)
1/4 cup oil
1-1/2 cups cornmeal

1/2 cup whole wheat pastry flour
1 teaspoon baking soda
1/2 teaspoon sea salt

Preheat oven to 400 F. Oil a muffin tin.
In a medium-sized bowl, combine all the liquid ingredients; mix well. In another bowl, combine all the dry ingredients. Add the dry mixture to the liquid and stir well. Bake for 25 minutes—test with toothpick, placed in center of muffin; if it comes out dry, muffins are ready.

WHOLE WHEAT MUFFINS
Yields 1 dozen

2 cups whole wheat flour
1/2 cup bran
1 teaspoon baking soda
1 teaspoon cinnamon

1/3 cup oil
1/2 cup sorghum
1 teaspoon vanilla
4 tablespoons quick soymilk
(see recipe)

Preheat oven to 400 F. Combine the dry ingredients in a medium sized bowl; combine the liquid ingredients in a large bowl. Blend the dry ingredients into the liquid mixture; oil a muffin tin. Spoon the batter into the cups until 3/4 full. Bake for 20 minutes or until golden brown.

VARIATION

Add grated apple, grated carrot, raisins, nuts, or berries to the batter.

MOOKIES
Yields 15 mookies

This is a cross between muffins and cookies.

2 cups whole wheat flour
1/2 cup raisins
1 teaspoon cinnamon
1/2 teaspoon baking soda

1 cup soymilk (see recipe)
1/3 cup oil
1/2 cup sorghum
1 teaspoon vanilla

Preheat oven to 400 F. Combine the dry ingredients in a medium sized bowl. Combine all the liquid ingredients in a large bowl; add the dry ingredients. Drop the batter by the tablespoonful onto an oiled cookie sheet. Bake for 20 minutes.

VARIATION

Bran Mookies: Substitute 1-1/2 cups bran for 1-1/2 cups of the flour.

CRACKERS
Yields 15 crackers

1/2 tablespoon yeast   1/4 cup oil
1/2 cup warm water   1/8 teaspoon sea salt
2 cups flour (whole wheat or pastry)   1/8 teaspoon garlic powder
1/2 cup nutritional yeast

Dissolve the yeast in the water in a large bowl. Mix in the oil, flour, nutritional yeast and seasoning. Add enough water to make a soft dough. Allow to stand for 1 hour.

Roll the dough out to 1/4 inch thick. Cut into squares and place on an oiled baking sheet. Allow to rise for 15 to 25 minutes.

Preheat oven to 350 F. Bake for 10 to 15 minutes, turning once, until crispy. Serve with soup, guacamole, or any cold salad.

RAISIN OATMEAL BREAD
Yields 3 loaves

1-1/2 cups boiling water   3 tablespoons oil
1 cup rolled oats   2 teaspoons sea salt
1 tablespoon dry active yeast   2 cups raisins soaked
2 cups lukewarm water   in 4 cups water
3/4 cup sorghum   9 to 10 cups whole wheat flour

Combine the boiling water and oats in a medium sized bowl. Allow to stand for 30 minutes. In a large bowl, dissolve the yeast in the warm water. Add the sorghum, oil and salt; add the oat mixture and drained raisins. Work in enough flour to form a medium soft dough. Turn the dough onto a floured board and knead for approximately 10 minutes until smooth. Place the dough in a clean oiled bowl, turn and oil the top. Cover the dough with a clean dishcloth; place in a warm place, and allow to rise for about an hour, or until doubled in bulk.

Turn the dough onto a floured board, and knead for 10 minutes more, adding more flour if needed. Divide and shape the dough into 3 loaves. Place in loaf pans, sprinkled with cornmeal on the bottom. Cover and allow to rise for approximately an hour, or until doubled in bulk. Preheat oven to 400 F. Bake the loaves for 5 minutes; reduce oven to 350 F., and bake for 40 minutes longer, or till loaves sound hollow when tapped. Brush the tops of finished loaves with oil to make a soft crust.

LIGHT WHOLE WHEAT BREAD
Yields 2 loaves

2-1/2 cups lukewarm water
1-1/2 tablespoons yeast
1 teaspoon sorghum
3 tablespoons oil

1 teaspoon sea salt
4-1/2 cups whole wheat flour
1-1/2 cups whole wheat pastry flour
2 cups soy flour

In a large bowl, combine the water and yeast. Add the sorghum, oil, and salt. Add 3 cups of the whole wheat flour, 1 cup whole wheat pastry flour, and 1 cup soy flour; blend well. Cover with a cloth and allow to rise for 1 hour.

Add the remaining 1-1/2 cups whole wheat flour, 1/2 cup whole wheat pastry flour, and 1 cup soy flour; mix well. Turn the dough onto a floured board and knead for 10 minutes. Form into 2 loaves. Place in bread pans sprinkled with dried breadcrumbs or cornmeal to prevent sticking. Allow to rise for 1 to 1-1/2 hours.

Preheat oven to 325 F. Bake the loaves for 50 minutes, rotating loaves between the racks after 25 minutes.

VARIATION

Cinnamon Filling

This technique can be used with any whole wheat bread recipe. It takes place after you knead the dough, and after rising, punching down, prior to forming it into loaves.

1/4 cup sorghum
1/4 cup date sugar
2 teaspoons vanilla

1/4 teaspoon cinnamon
1-1/2 cups raisins, soaked
   in water for 5 to 10 minutes

Combine the sorghum, date sugar and vanilla in a small bowl. Flatten each loaf by hand until it is 1/4 inch to 1/2 inch thick. Drain the raisins. Spread the liquid filling over each loaf; sprinkle raisins and cinnamon on top. Roll up each loaf. Fold into a horseshoe shape if desired and place in a casserole dish or on a cookie sheet. For a crisper crust, brush 2 tablespoons oil combined with 1 tablespoon sorghum on top of each loaf for the last 5 minutes of baking time, at same temperature.

EASY PUMPERNICKEL BREAD
Yields 2 loaves

3 tablespoons active dry yeast
2 cups warm water
4 teaspoons sea salt
1/2 cup molasses

2 tablespoons caraway seeds
2 tablespoons oil
2 cups rye flour
4 cups whole wheat flour

Preheat oven at 350 F. Dissolve yeast in water. Stir in salt, molasses, and caraway seeds. Add oil and 1/2 of the flour, mix well, add remaining flour. Knead until smooth. Place in an oiled bowl and let rise until double, approximately 1 hour. Punch down, divide in half and shape, and put into loaf pans. Let rise 30 to 40 minutes, and bake for 50 to 55 minutes.

PUMPERNICKEL BREAD
Yields 2 loaves

2-1/2 cups whole wheat flour
1-1/2 cups rye flour
1/2 cup bran
1 tablespoon active dry yeast
1-1/2 tablespoons caraway seeds
1 teaspoon sea salt

2 teaspoons powdered dark
   coffee substitute (such as Postum)
2-1/2 tablespoons cider vinegar
1-1/3 cups water
2 tablespoons carob powder
4 tablespoons sorghum
4 tablespoons oil

Combine 1-1/2 cups of the whole wheat flour; the rye flour, bran, yeast, caraway seeds, and salt in a large bowl. Stir well. In a saucepan, combine the remaining ingredients, except flour; heat over medium heat until warm, stirring often. Gradually add to the flour mixture; beat well. Add the remaining flour; stir. Turn dough onto floured board. Knead for 10 minutes, until smooth and elastic; add more flour if needed. Oil the bowl and return kneaded dough to it; oil top of dough. Cover and allow to rise for 1-1/2 hours.

Turn dough onto a floured board and knead for 5 minutes. Divide into 2 loaves. Oil and flour 2 loaf pans. Add the loaves. Cover and allow to rise for 30 minutes.

Preheat oven to 350 F. Bake loaves for 35 minutes, until hollow sounding when tapped on top, and a knife comes out clean when inserted in the middle of the loaf.

WHOLE WHEAT BREAD
Yields 3 loaves

2 cups soymilk,
   scalded and cooled (see recipe)
1/2 cup sorghum
2 tablespoons yeast,
   dissolved in 1/4 cup warm water

1/4 cup oil
1 tablespoon sea salt
4 cups whole wheat flour
4 cups whole wheat pastry flour

Combine the ingredients in a large bowl and mix well. Turn the dough onto a floured board; knead until elastic, approximately 15 minutes. Place dough in an oiled bowl, cover with a clean cloth and allow to rise overnight or until double in bulk. Punch the dough down and allow to rise for 1-1/2 hours, punch the dough down again; shape into 3 loaves and place in oiled loaf pans. Allow to rise for approximately 1 hour or until the dough rises above the edges of the pan.

Preheat oven to 400 F. Bake loaves for 1 hour.

FLUFFY PUMPERNICKEL RAISIN BREAD
Yields 5 loaves

6 tablespoons yeast
4 cups warm water
3 teaspoons sea salt
1 cup molasses
1-1/2 cups raisins, washed

4 tablespoons oil
2 cups oat flour*
10 to 12 cups whole wheat flour
2 tablespoons caraway seeds

In a large bowl, add the yeast to warm water. Let stand 5 minutes. Add salt, molasses, raisins and oil. Mix well. Add remaining ingredients a little at a time; stirring each time you add.
 Knead until smooth. Place in oiled bowl. Cover and let rise 1-1/2 hours. Punch down. Knead 10 minutes. Shape into loaves.
 Preheat oven at 350 F. Bake for 45 minutes.

*To make oat flour: Place 2 cups rolled oats in blender. Blend at medium speed for 45 seconds, or until it becomes a powder.

VARIATION

Save one loaf worth of dough, omitting caraway seeds, to make delicious sweet rolls:

Filling For Rolls

3/4 cup sunflower seeds
   (lightly roasted in pan)
3/4 cup raisins, finely chopped
1 cup apples, finely chopped
3/4 cup sorghum

3/4 cup oats
Juice of one lemon
Cinnamon to taste
1/4 cup sesame seeds,
   lightly roasted

Mix all ingredients except sesame seeds. Roll dough out in a circle 1/4-inch thick, and spread filling evenly over entire circle. Cut into pie-slice shapes of triangles, and roll up from either end. Dip bottoms in sesame seeds and bake at bread temperature for 20 to 30 minutes.

FLUFFY DINNER ROLLS
Yields 12 rolls

2 tablespoons dry active yeast
1/3 cup sweetener (sorghum)
1-1/3 cups warm soymilk
1/2 cup oil

3 cups whole wheat pastry flour
2-1/2 cups whole wheat flour
1 teaspoon sea salt
3/4 teaspoon baking soda

Place the yeast in a large bowl; add the sorghum and warm milk, stirring until yeast is dissolved. Add the oil and stir. Add 3 cups of the pastry flour and stir well. Cover the bowl with a towel and allow to rise for 30 minutes. Stir in the remaining flour, salt and baking soda; cover and allow to rise for 30 minutes more.
 Preheat oven to 400 F. Oil 2 cookie sheets. Turn the dough onto a floured board and divide into 12 equal parts. Shape according to whim, into circles and fold in half; or into balls. Place rolls on the cookie sheets. They will double in size while baking. Bake for 20 minutes or until golden.

EASY WHOLE WHEAT BREAD
Yields 2 loaves

2 teaspoons sea salt
3 tablespoons oil
2 tablespoons sorghum
2 cups soymilk, hot (see recipe)

1 tablespoon active dry yeast
4 tablespoons lukewarm water
6 cups whole wheat or whole wheat
   pastry flour (or some of each)

In a large bowl, add salt, oil and sorghum. Pour the hot soymilk on top. Mix, and cool to lukewarm. Dissolve the yeast in the water; and add to soymilk mixture. Mix in flour, knead for about 10 minutes, until smooth. Place dough in oiled bowl. Oil the top; cover, let rise for 2 hours. Punch down, turn over, and let rise another half hour.

Separate into 2 pieces and let sit 5 minutes. Roll out and fold to shape into a loaf. Place loaf seam-side-down, in floured bread pan. Cover and let rise for 1 hour.

Preheat oven to 400 F.

Bake for 30 minutes or until lightly golden on top. It will sound hollow when tapped.

Hint: For a soft crust, brush top with oil when finished.

DEER'S BREAD
Yields 2 loaves

2 tablespoons dry active yeast
3 cups lukewarm water
1 cup sorghum
1/4 cup safflower oil
1 teaspoon sea salt

1/2 cup sesame seeds
1 cup raisins (optional)
6 cups whole wheat flour
1 cup oats
1 cup rye flour (optional)

Stir the yeast into the warm water in a large bowl to dissolve. Set aside for 5 minutes. Add the sorghum, oil, salt, seeds and raisins. Stir in 4 cups of the flour, mixing well. Add the oats and rye flour. Add the remaining flour and mix until slightly sticky. Turn onto a floured board and knead for approximately 15 minutes. Place dough in an oiled bowl; allow to rise for 1-1/2 hours.

Punch dough down and knead for 5 minutes. Divide into 2 equal loaves. Sprinkle corn meal or bran over the bottom of 2 loaf pans to prevent sticking. Place loaves in pans. Allow to rise for 1 hour.

Preheat oven to 350 F. Bake loaves for 40 minutes until hollow sounding when tapped on top.

GOOD BREAD
Yields 2 loaves

5 cups whole wheat flour
1 cup cornmeal
2 tablespoons active dry yeast
2 teaspoons sea salt

2 cups warm water
5 tablespoons safflower oil
1/2 cup sorghum
Sprinkle of cornmeal or bran

In a large bowl, combine 2 cups of the flour, cornmeal, yeast and salt. Add the water, oil and sorghum. Stir well for 3 minutes. Add enough of the remaining flour to form a stiff dough. Turn onto a floured board and knead for 10 minutes, until no longer sticky. Place in an oiled bowl; oil top of dough lightly, cover and allow to rise for 1-1/2 hours in a warm place.

Punch the dough down. Knead for 3 to 4 minutes. Divide into 2 equal parts Sprinkle the bottom and sides of two loaf pans with bran or cornmeal to prevent sticking. Cover and allow to rise for 40 minutes.

Preheat oven to 350 F. Bake the loaves for 45 to 50 minutes.

"How can I teach your children gentleness and
mercy to the weak, and reverence for life, which
in its nakedness and excess, is still a gleam
of God's Omnipotence, when by your laws, your
actions and your speech, you contradict the very
things I teach?"...

"Among the noblest in the land—
Though man may count himself the least—
That man I honor and revere,
Who withour favor, without fear,
In the great city dares to stand,
The friend of every friendless beast."

Henry W. Longfellow

THE WORLD'S NEED

So many gods, so many creeds,
So many paths that wind and wind,
While just the art of being kind
Is all the sad world needs.

I am the voice of the voiceless;
Through me, the dumb shall speak;
Till the deaf world's ear be made to hear
The cry of the wordless weak.
From street, from cage and from kennel,
From jungle and stall, the wail
Of my tortured kin proclaims the sin
Of the mighty against the frail.

For love is the true religion,
And love is the law sublime;
And all that is wrought, where love is not
Will die at the touch of time.
Oh, shame on the mothers of mortals
Who have not stopped to teach
Of the sorrow that lies in dear, dumb eyes,
The sorrow that has no speech.

The same Power formed the sparrow
That fashioned man— the King;
The God of the whole gave a living soul
To furred and to feathered thing.
And I am my brother's keeper.
And I will fight his fight;
And speak the word for beast and bird
Till the world shall set things right.

Ella Wheeler Wilcox

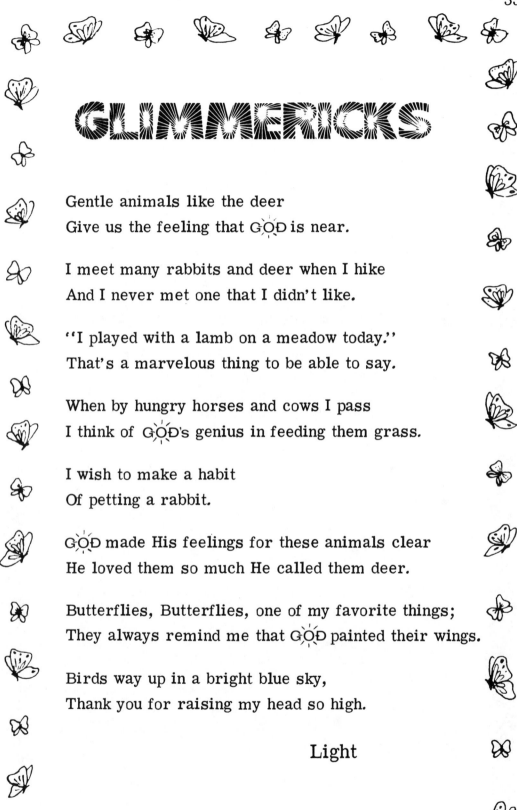

GLIMMERICKS

Gentle animals like the deer
Give us the feeling that GOD is near.

I meet many rabbits and deer when I hike
And I never met one that I didn't like.

"I played with a lamb on a meadow today."
That's a marvelous thing to be able to say.

When by hungry horses and cows I pass
I think of GOD's genius in feeding them grass.

I wish to make a habit
Of petting a rabbit.

GOD made His feelings for these animals clear
He loved them so much He called them deer.

Butterflies, Butterflies, one of my favorite things;
They always remind me that GOD painted their wings.

Birds way up in a bright blue sky,
Thank you for raising my head so high.

Light

"The unpardonable forgetfulness in which the lower animals have hitherto been left by the moralists of Europe is well known. It is pretended that the beasts have no rights. They persuade themselves that our conduct in regard to them has nothing to do with morals or that we have no duties towards animals; a doctrine revolting, gross, and barbarous, peculiar to the West.

"I know of no more beautiful prayer than that which the Hindus of old used in closing their public spectacles. It was: 'May all that have Life be delivered from suffering!' "

Arthur Schopenhauer

Soups and Sandwiches

CABBAGE SOUP
Serves 6

2 tablespoons oil
3 garlic cloves, diced
2 large onions, diced
3 carrots, diced
1 head cabbage, shredded
8 cups vegetable stock or water

1 apple, grated
3 tablespoons tamari
1/2 teaspoon garlic powder
1/2 teaspoon basil
1/2 teaspoon parsley

Heat the oil in a soup pot over medium heat; add the garlic and onions, and saute for 5 minutes. Add the remaining vegetables and cook for 5 minutes, until soft; add the stock, apple, and seasonings. Cook for 1 hour.

ONION SOUP
Serves 6

1/8 to 1/4 cup oil
7 garlic cloves, diced
8 large onions, sliced
8 cups stock
2 tablespoons soy powder
1 cup tomato puree or juice
3 tablespoons fresh parsely, chopped

1 teaspoon sea salt
1 teaspoon tarragon
1/3 cup tamari
1/4 teaspoon garlic powder
1/4 teaspoon basil
1/4 teaspoon oregano

Heat the oil in a soup pot; add the garlic, and saute for 1 minute until golden. Add the onions, and continue to saute until tender; add the stock. Combine the soy powder and tomato puree; add to the pot. Cook over low heat for 10 minutes; add the seasonings. Reduce heat, cover, and simmer for 20 minutes.

If desired, toast whole wheat bread, cut into cubes, and serve in soup; or sprinkle nutritional yeast on top.

TOMATO SOUP
Serves 6 to 8

10 cups tomato stock (tomato juice or cooked tomatoes squeezed through a strainer)
2 tablespoons oil
4 garlic cloves, diced
4 to 5 onions, sliced
2 celery stalks, diced
1/2 cup tamari

1 teaspoon basil
1 teaspoon oregano
1 teaspoon garlic powder
1/2 teaspoon sea salt
2 sprigs of fresh parsley
2 tablespoons sorghum
3 tablespoons soy powder

Heat the oil in a soup pot, add the garlic and onion, and saute for 5 minutes. Add the celery, and saute for 3 minutes more, until tender; add the stock and seasonings. Cook for 30 minutes over medium-low heat; dilute the soy powder in 2 cups of soup stock, and add to the soup. Add the sorghum, and re-season to taste. Cook for 30 minutes more over low heat. Especially delicious served the next day.

GARDEN VEGETABLE SOUP
Serves 6

2 tablespoons oil
2 onions, diced
3 carrots, sliced
3 celery stalks with tops, diced
3 potatoes, cubed
3 beets, cubed
1 cup string beans, chopped
1/2 head cabbage, shredded
1 bay leaf

1/2 teaspoon garlic powder
1/2 teaspoon sea salt
Dash of red pepper
3 garlic cloves, diced
3 teaspoons tamari
8 cups of water or stock
3 cups fresh peas
1/2 cup fresh parsley, chopped

Heat the oil in a soup pot over medium-high heat; add the onions and saute for 5 minutes until tender. Add the remaining vegetables and seasonings except the peas and parsley. Add the stock and bring to a boil; reduce heat and simmer for 20 minutes; add the peas and cook for 10 minutes more, until all the vegetables are tender. Do not over cook. Garnish with parsley before serving.

BARLEY SOUP
Serves 4 to 6

7 cups water or stock
1/2 cup barley
1 carrot, sliced
3 celery stalks, diced
3 onions, diced
5 tablespoons tamari
3 garlic cloves, diced

2 cups tomatoes, peeled and
  cut into chunks
1/2 teaspoon sea salt
1/2 teaspoon garlic powder
1/2 teaspoon basil
1/2 teaspoon oregano
1/2 teaspoon parsley

In a large soup pot, combine the water and barley; cook over medium heat for approximately 40 minutes. Add the remaining ingredients. Reduce heat to low and cook for approximately 45 minutes more. Garnish with parsley and serve.

MISO SOUP
Serves 4 to 6

2 tablespoons oil
4 garlic cloves, diced
2 large onions, diced
2 carrots, cut into large pieces
2 celery stalks, diced
7 cups vegetable stock
1 cup small lima beans
1/4 teaspoon oregano

1/4 teaspoon garlic powder
1/4 teaspoon sea salt
1/4 teaspoon parsley
1/8 teaspoon paprika
2 tablespoons tamari
1 cup whole wheat or
  spinach noodles (optional)
4 to 6 tablespoons of miso paste

In a soup pot, heat the oil over medium-high heat; add the garlic, onions, carrots, and celery; saute for 7 minutes till golden brown. Add the stock, beans, and spices; cook for 1 to 2 hours over medium-low heat. Add the noodles, and cook until tender.

Dilute the miso paste in 1 cup of warm stock; add to the soup, and simmer for 30 minutes.

GARDEN VEGETABLE SOUP A LA GRAIN
Serves 6 to 8

2 tablespoons oil
3 garlic cloves, diced
3 large onions, diced
2 celery stalks, diced
2 carrots, diced
3 potatoes, diced (unpeeled)
2 cups any green vegetable
   (celery tops, cabbage leaves,
   swiss chard, beet greens, etc.)
5 tablespoons tamari

1 cup corn kernels
10 to 12 cups stock or water
1/2 cup any cooked grain
   (rice, kasha, millet, etc.)
1/2 teaspoon dill
1/2 teaspoon basil
1/2 teaspoon sea salt
1/2 teaspoon oregano
1/2 teaspoon garlic powder
1/2 teaspoon parsley

Heat the oil in a large soup pot over medium heat; add the garlic, onions, celery, carrots, and potatoes; saute for 4 minutes. Cut the green leafy vegetables into bite-size pieces, and add to the mixture. Saute for approximately 3 minutes, gradually adding the tamari and corn, until the vegetables are soft. Add the stock, grain, and seasonings. Cook for 2 to 3 hours over low heat.

VARIATION

When soup is done, dilute 5 tablespoons of soy powder in 1 cup of stock; mix into soup to add flavor and thickness.

For a heartier flavor, more protein and nourishment, dilute 3 tablespoons of miso in 1 cup of stock. Add after cooking soup. Never boil miso, as it loses nutrients.

TOMATO VEGETABLE SOUP
Serves 6 to 8

1/4 cup oil
2 garlic cloves, diced
2 onions, cut into chunks
1 large potato, cut into chunks
2 carrots, cut into chunks
2 celery stalks, sliced
1/2 cup broccoli, chopped
1/2 cup cauliflower, chopped

1/2 cup fresh green peas
10 to 12 cups tomato stock
1/2 cup tamari
1 teaspoon parsley
1/2 teaspoon dill weed
1/2 teaspoon garlic powder
1/2 teaspoon sweet basil
1/2 teaspoon sea salt

In a large soup pot, heat the oil over medium heat; add the garlic, onion, potato, carrots, and celery, and saute for 5 minutes. Season with about half of the spices. Add the remaining vegetables and cook for 3 to 4 minutes. Add the stock; reduce heat and simmer for 1 hour.

Add the remaining seasonings, to taste. Cook 10 minutes more until the vegetables are soft. Spoon approximately 1/2 of the vegetables, especially carrots and potatoes, from the soup into a blender; add 2 cups stock and puree for 1 minute. Return the mixture to the pot. Cook for 1 hour more over low heat, and serve.

CORN CHOWDER
Serves 6 to 8

3 tablespoons oil
3 large onions, diced
4 garlic cloves, minced
5 cups fresh corn kernels,
(cut from the cob)
3 tablespoons soy powder
2-1/2 quarts water
2 to 3 carrots, sliced

3 to 4 potatoes, diced
3 tablespoons tamari
1 teaspoon sea salt
1 teaspoon garlic powder
1/2 teaspoon basil
1/2 teaspoon thyme
4 tablespoons tahini

In a large pot, heat the oil over medium-high heat; add the onions and garlic, and saute for 3 to 4 minutes. Mix in the corn; saute for 3 to 4 minutes more. In a blender, combine 4/5 of the corn and onion mixture with the soy powder and water. It will take a few blender fulls to do it all; each time use 1/3 of entire mixture. A thick creamy texture is desired. Put back into pot, add remaining ingredients except tahini and cook over very low heat (it has a tendency to stick) for 2 hours, stirring often. Remove 1 cup of soup; and mix the tahini in, and return it to the pot. Cook for 1/2 hour. Serve.

SPLIT PEA SOUP
Serves 6 to 8

2 cups green split peas
8 cups water or vegetable stock
1 onion, diced
2 celery stalks, diced
2 large carrots, sliced
1 turnip, diced
1 potato, diced
1/3 cup tamari

1/2 teaspoon garlic powder
1 teaspoon sweet basil
1/4 teaspoon sea salt
1/4 teaspoon marjoram
1/8 teaspoon red pepper
2 garlic cloves, diced
2 bay leaves
1/4 cup barley

Combine the peas and the water in a large saucepan; place over medium heat and bring to boil. Reduce heat; add the onion, celery, one carrot, turnip, potato, tamari, and seasonings. Cook for 1 hour, till the peas and all vegetables are soft. Remove the bay leaves.

Transfer mixture to a blender, and blend at high speed for 1 minute, until well mixed. This will take 3 to 4 blenders full. Add 1 clove of diced garlic while blending.

Pour back into pot. Add the barley, the remaining carrot and the bay leaves; season to taste. Cook over low heat for 2 hours, stirring often.

CREAM OF CAULIFLOWER SOUP
Serves 5

2 cups cooked brown rice
5 cups vegetable stock
1 head cauliflower, chopped
2 stalks celery, chopped
2 tablespoons tahini

1/4 cup tamari
1/2 teaspoon garlic powder
1/4 teaspoon basil
1/8 teaspoon red pepper

In a blender, combine the cooked rice with the stock; blend at high speed for 1 minute, until creamy. It will take a few blender loads to do it all. Each time use 1/3 the entire mixture. Add 1/2 of the cauliflower and blend at high speed for 1 minute.

Pour mixture into a large soup pot. Place over medium heat; add the rest of the cauliflower and remaining ingredients. Cook for approximately 1 hour, until the cauliflower is tender.

BROTH
Serves 6

10 cups stock or water
1/4 head cabbage, shredded
3 potatoes, cut into chunks
2 carrots, cut into chunks
2 onions, cut into chunks
2 celery stalks, diced
2 beets, cut into chunks
2 turnips, cut into chunks

5 garlic cloves, diced
5 tablespoons tamari
1/4 cup parsley, chopped
1 teaspoon oregano
1 teaspoon basil
1/2 teaspoon garlic powder
1/2 teaspoon dill weed
Dash of cayenne pepper

In a large stainless steel pot, combine the stock and all the vegetables and seasonings (use fresh herbs if possible). Cook over low heat for 3 to 4 hours.

Season to taste. Strain the broth out or serve with vegetables. Makes a good hot drink on cool days, or when a cold is coming on. Serve with a sprinkle of nutritional yeast.

VARIATION

Add chunks of tomato to broth before cooking.

MUSHROOM BARLEY SOUP
Serves 6 to 8

2 tablespoons oil
2 medium onions, diced
2 garlic cloves, diced
2 celery stalks, diced
1 pound fresh mushrooms, chopped
1 cup barley
1/2 cup tamari

1/2 teaspoon garlic powder
1/2 teaspoon sea salt
1 teaspoon parsley, chopped
1 teaspoon dill
10 cups water or stock
2 carrots, diced

In a large soup pot, heat the oil over medium-high heat; add the onions, garlic, celery, and mushrooms, and saute for 4 minutes. Add seasonings, barley, and the water. Reduce heat and simmer for 2 to 3 hours, adding the carrots approximately 45 minutes before soup is finished. To thin soup, add more water.

LENTIL SOUP
Serves 6

2 tablespoons oil
2 garlic cloves, diced
2 large onions, cut into chunks
2 celery stalks, diced
1 carrot, sliced
1 potato, cut into chunks
4 tablespoons tamari
1/2 teaspoon garlic powder

1/2 teaspoon basil
1/2 teaspoon paprika
1/2 teaspoon sea salt
1/4 teaspoon cumin powder
1/4 teaspoon oregano
10 cups of water or stock
3 tomatoes, cut into chunks
1-1/2 cups lentils

In a large soup pot, heat the oil over medium-high heat; add the garlic, onions, celery, carrots, and potatoes; saute for 7 minutes, until tender, adding the tamari and half of the seasonings while sauteing.

Add the water, tomatoes, and lentils. Cook over medium heat until it boils; reduce heat, and cook for 1 hour. Add remaining seasonings to taste. Cook for another hour.

NAVY BEAN SOUP
Serves 6 to 8

2 cups navy, great northern,
   or pinto beans
Approximately 10 cups water
1/3 cup oil
1/4 cup tamari
2 onions, diced
1 teaspoon garlic powder

1 teaspoon sea salt
Dash of red pepper
1 carrot, sliced
1 stalk celery, diced
8 garlic cloves, diced
2 bay leaves

Soak the beans overnight in water to cover. The next day, rinse the beans and place in a large pot; cover with water and place over medium heat. Add the oil, tamari, 1 of the diced onions, 4 garlic cloves, and seasonings.

Cook for approximately an hour; add the carrots, celery, the remaining onion, and 4 more garlic cloves. Cook for approximately 1 hour more, until the carrots and beans are tender. Remove bay leaves before serving.

VARIATION

The liquid can be drained off and the beans served as a side dish or main course.

PIZZA SANDWICH
Serves 1

1 slice whole wheat bread
2 to 3 tomato slices
1 onion slice
1 teaspoon sesame seeds

3 tablespoons tahini dressing
   (see recipe)
1 teaspoon nutritional yeast

Warm the bread in a toaster oven; before it is browned, remove it and spread with tahini dressing. Layer with the tomato, the onion, sesame seeds, tahini dressing and nutritional yeast on top; place under a broiler or in a toaster oven, and toast for 3 to 4 minutes until golden brown.

Great for lunch.

VARIATION

Add 2 teaspoons tomato sauce to the tahini dressing.

SPROUT SANDWICH
Serves 1

2 slices whole wheat bread
2 tablespoons tahini
1/2 tomato, sliced
1/2 avocado, sliced

2 onion slices
Handful of sprouts
   (alfalfa or sunflower)

Spread the tahini on one slice of the bread; layer the remaining ingredients. Top with remaining slice of bread.

VARIATION

Replace filling ingredients with lettuce, cucumber, shredded cabbage, and sliced tofu.

PEANUT BUTTER DELIGHT
Serves 1

2 slices whole wheat bread
4 tablespoons peanut butter

1 banana, sliced
1/4 cup raisins

Spread the peanut butter on both bread slices. Top one slice with banana slices, raisins and remaining bread.

VARIATION

Substitute any nut butter, instead of peanut butter.

Top filling with a light coating of sorghum.

MEXICAN STYLE MILLET
Serves 1

2 slices whole wheat bread
1 tablespoon tahini
1 millet burger (see recipe)
1/4 small onion, chopped

1/2 cup lettuce, shredded
Handful of sprouts
1/2 tomato, sliced
1 tablespoon guacamole (see recipe)

Coat one slice of bread with a thin layer of tahini. Place millet burger on top; garnish with onion, shredded lettuce, sprouts and sliced tomato. Top with guacamole.
   Great lunch!

"You are not living in a private world all your own. Everything you say and do and think has its effect on everything around you. For example, if you feel and say loudly enough that it is an infernal shame to keep larks and other wild song-birds in cages, you will infallibly infect a number of other people with that sentiment, and in course of time, those people who feel as you do will become so numerous that larks, thrushes, blackbirds and linnets will no longer be caught and kept in cages.

"How do you imagine it ever came about that bulls and bears and badgers are no longer baited, cocks no longer openly encouraged to tear each other to pieces, donkeys no longer beaten to pulp?

"Only because people went about shouting that these things made them uncomfortable.

"When a thing exists which you really abhor, I wish you would remember a little whether in letting it strictly alone, you are minding your own business on principle, or simply because it is comfortable to do so."

John Gallsworthy

"The day may come when the rest of the animal creation may acquire those rights which never could have been withholden from them but by the hand of tyranny. The question is not 'Can they REASON, nor can they TALK, but can they SUFFER?' "

Jeremy Bentham

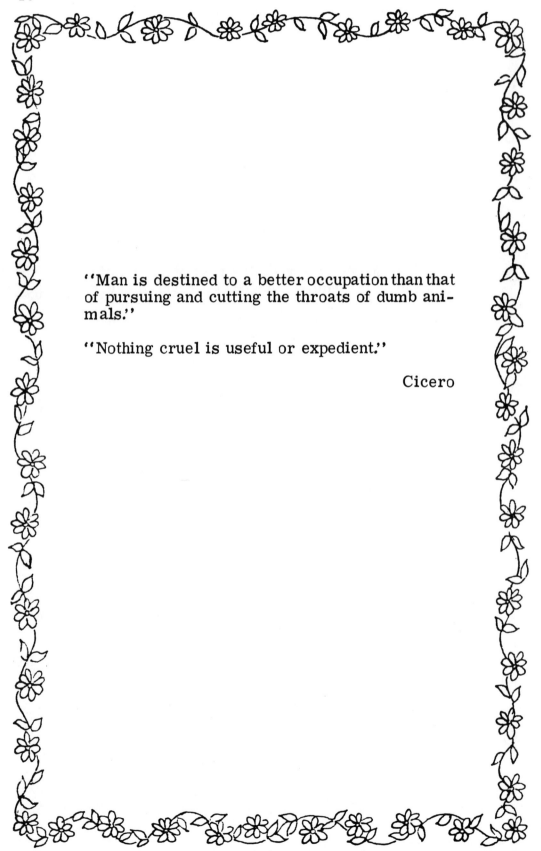

''Man is destined to a better occupation than that
of pursuing and cutting the throats of dumb animals.''

''Nothing cruel is useful or expedient.''

Cicero

"Personally, I would not give a fig for any man's religion whose horse or dog do not feel its benefits. Life in any form is our perpetual responsibility. Its abuse degrades those who practice it. Its rightful usage is a signal token of genuine manhood. If there be a superintending justice, surely it takes account of the injuries and sufferings of helpless yet animate creation. Let us be perfectly clear about the spirituality of the issue before us. We have abolished human bondage because it cursed those who imposed it. It is now our bounden duty to abolish the futile and ferocious oppression of those creatures of our common Father which share with man the mystery of life...

"I close as I began, with the reminder that this theme is nothing if not spiritual; an acid test of our relation to the Deity of love and compassion.' "

Rev. Dr. S. Parkes Cadman

"Tenderness and mercy and gentility, and all the spiritual qualities that set man off so greatly from beasts of prey, are lacking in the lion, tiger, wolf and other carnivora. The claim that man has evolved to such a high mental plane and spiritual plane that he must have meat is exactly the opposite of the facts. He must crush and harden his higher nature in order to hunt and fish and prey."

Dr. H. M. Shelton

Salads

SPROUTING

Seeds that may be used in these recipes include: alfalfa, mung, lentil, wheat berry, sunflower, buckwheat, chick-peas, soybeans (can sprout by methods 1 and 2).

1) SPROUTING ON TRAYS

Rinse approximately 1/4 cup of sprout seeds and place in a bowl; add water to cover. Allow to soak overnight. The following morning, drain off the liquid (good for watering plants).

Line a flat tray with paper towels or mesh screening. Spread the seeds in a thin layer on the towel; cover the seeds with a layer of paper towel and sprinkle with water. All the seeds must be moistened. Place the tray in an undisturbed dark area. Check the tray twice a day to be sure the sprouts remain damp, but not wet.

By the second day you will see little sprouts beginning to pop. By the third day or fourth day most of the sprouts (depending on the kind) will be mature and ready. Expose the matured sprouts to a few hours of sunlight; this gives them the opportunity to develop chlorophyll and gives them sun energy.

2) SPROUTING IN A JAR

Place 1/8 cup of sprout seeds in a 2-quart, wide-mouthed jar; add water to cover. Cover top of jar with a piece of cheese cloth or some type of small mesh screening. Allow to soak overnight.

The following day, rinse the sprouts and drain well. Lie the jar on its side and spread the seeds out thinly to cover as much of the inner surface of the jar as possible. Place the jar in an undisturbed dark place.

Starting the next day after that, rinse the sprouts twice a day. After 3 or 4 days, place the jar in the sunlight for a few hours to prepare sprouts for eating. Then store sprouts in the refrigerator, unless using them right away.

3) EARTH SPROUTING

Fill your trays (8'' x 12'') with garden soil. Sprinkle 1 cup sprout seeds liberally over the soil. Cover with 1/4-inch of soil. Lightly water the soil. Store the trays indoors or outdoors, watering every day or every other day to prevent drying out.

When the sprouts have grown 4'' tall, begin snipping and using them in salads or sandwiches; don't let them grow too long, as their nutritional value decreases.

This method is particularly good for wheat berries, sunflower seeds, buckwheat lettuce, and rye sprouts. Wheat and rye berries regrow; they can be snipped twice.

GARDEN SALAD
Serves 10

This salad is one of our very favorites, and is best when the vegetables are freshly picked.

2 heads loose-leaf lettuce
1/2 head cabbage, shredded
6 Swiss chard leaves, chopped
3 Chinese cabbage leaves,
    finely shredded
1 head cauliflower,
    broken into flowerettes
3 stalks broccoli, chopped

1 zucchini, diced
5 large spinach leaves, chopped
3 carrots, diced
1 red pepper, diced
4 scallion tops, diced
1 beet, diced or grated
2 kohlrabi, diced

Wash all the vegetables thoroughly. Cut all the greens into bite-size pieces. Combine all the ingredients in a large bowl; toss, add dressing, chill and serve.

VARIATION

Add sunflower seeds or cooked chick-peas to the finished salad.

SPINACH MUSHROOM SALAD
Serves 6

1 garlic clove, mashed
1 pound fresh spinach, chopped
1/2 pound fresh mushrooms, sliced
5 tomatoes, cut into chunks

1 head lettuce, shredded
1/4 head cabbage, shredded
2 peppers, sliced
1 garlic clove, diced

Rub large wooden bowl with the mashed garlic. Add all the ingredients except the tomatoes, and toss. Chill for 1 to 2 hours, to allow garlic to permeate the salad.
Serve with oil and vinegar or your favorite dressing. Top with tomatoes.

SPROUT SALAD
Serves 4

4 cups of sprouts (any combination
    of alfalfa, mung, sunflower seed,
    lentil, etc.)
1 medium onion, diced
1/2 head lettuce, cut into chunks

1/4 head cabbage, shredded
1 cucumber, diced
1 green pepper, diced
3 tomatoes, diced

Combine all the ingredients in a large bowl; toss. Add dressing; chill and serve.

GREEN SALAD
Serves 6 to 8

3 cups mixed lettuce (romaine,
bibb, loose-leaf, iceberg)
1 cup cabbage, shredded
2 green peppers, diced
1 avocado, peeled and diced
1/2 cup kale, chopped
1 cup spinach, chopped
1/4 cup chives, diced

1 medium zucchini, diced
2 kohlrabi, diced
1 cup Swiss chard, diced
1/4 cup comfrey, diced
1/2 cup string beans, diced
1/2 cup fresh peas
1 cup alfalfa sprouts

Combine all the ingredients in a large bowl, tearing the lettuce by hand to preserve freshness. Serve with your favorite dressing. If served in a wooden bowl, for extra zing rub the bowl with a fresh garlic clove before adding the salad.

AVOCADO SALAD PLATTER
Serves 6

1 head of lettuce
2 ripe avocados, peeled and sliced
1 onion, sliced in thin rings
2 8-ounce cakes tofu,
cut into 1-inch cubes

1 red pepper, sliced into strips
2 celery stalks, cut into sticks
1 carrot, cut into thin sticks
Flowerettes of 6 stalks of broccoli

Cover a large platter with lettuce leaves. Arrange the vegetables, avocados, and tofu in an alternating circle pattern on the platter. Serve with dressing or guacamole on the side.

Great for parties.

GUACAMOLE-AVOCADO WHIP
Serves 6 to 8

5 to 7 ripe avocados
1 celery stalk, diced fine
1 tomato, diced
1 small onion, diced

5 tablespoons tamari
1/2 teaspoon sea salt
1/4 teaspoon garlic powder
1/4 teaspoon kelp

Scoop out the avocados and mash in a large bowl. Mix in all the remaining ingredients.

VARIATION
Add 2 stalks of celery, diced.

STUFFED AVOCADOS
Serves 4

2 avocados
2 scallions or chives, diced
1 garden cucumber, cut into chunks
2 garden radishes, diced
2 tablespoons tamari
1/4 teaspoon sea salt

1/8 teaspoon garlic powder
1/2 teaspoon sesame meal
   (see recipe)
2 tablespoons nutritional yeast
1/2 cup sprouts (any kind)

Cut the avocados in half; remove the pits and gently scoop out the insides, leaving the shell intact. Mash the avocados; add the scallions, cucumber, radishes, and seasonings, and mix well. Fill the avocado shells with the mixture. Top with sesame meal, nutritional yeast, and sprouts.

APPLE, CARROT, RAISIN SALAD
Serves 4

4 apples, diced
4 carrots, grated
1 cup raisins

Juice of 1/4 lemon
1 tablespoon sorghum

Combine all the ingredients in a large bowl and mix well.

VARIATION
Add 1/2 cup tahini dressing.

RAW CARROT SALAD
Serves 6

2 pounds carrots, peeled and grated
1 onion, diced fine
2 stalks celery, diced
1/2 cup tahini
5 tablespoons tamari

1/2 teaspoon lemon juice, or
   1 teaspoon apple cider vinegar
1/4 teaspoon sea salt
1/4 teaspoon dill weed
1/4 teaspoon garlic powder

Combine all the ingredients in a large bowl, until creamy and crunchy. Chill and serve.

VARIATIONS
Add 1/2 cup sunflower seeds and/or 1/2 cup grated cabbage, or 2 grated beets, before chilling.

TOFU EGGLESS SALAD
Serves 4

2 12-ounce cakes tofu
2 tablespoons tamari
1 tablespoon oil
2 small onions, diced

2 celery stalks, diced
1/2 teaspoon sea salt
1 teaspoon turmeric
6 tablespoons nutritional yeast

In a medium-size bowl, mash the tofu; add the remaining ingredients and mix well. Refrigerate to keep cold.

Delicious with salad or as a sandwich.

OKARA SALAD
Serves 6

3 cups okara
3 cups stock or water
1 onion, diced
1 celery stalk, diced
1/4 cup nutritional yeast
2 tablespoons oil
Juice of 1/2 to 1 lemon or lime

3 to 5 tablespoons tamari
1 teaspoon sea salt
1/2 teaspoon oregano
1/2 teaspoon basil
1/2 teaspoon paprika
1/4 teaspoon dill seed

In a large bowl, combine the okara with the remaining ingredients. If too dry, add water. Refrigerate and serve cold.

CUCUMBER SALAD
Serves 5

6 to 8 cucumbers,
   peeled and sliced thin
2 onions, sliced into thin rings
1/2 cup apple cider vinegar
3 tablespoons tamari

1 tablespoon sorghum
1/2 cup water
1 garlic clove, diced
1 teaspoon sea salt

Combine all the ingredients in a large bowl. Chill for at least 2 hours, stirring occasionally.

VARIATION
Substitute sliced, steamed beets for the cucumbers.

SALADS

POTATO SALAD
Serves 8

potatoes, washed and cubed
reen peppers, chopped
arrots, chopped
talks celery, chopped
callions, diced
nion, diced
ups soy mayonnaise (see recipe)

1 teaspoon paprika
1 teaspoon basil
1 teaspoon sea salt
1 teaspoon oregano
1 teaspoon garlic powder
Dash of red pepper
4 tablespoons tamari

the potatoes, with water to cover, in a large saucepan over medium-
eat. Steam for 25 minutes, or until they are soft yet firm. Drain and

bine the cold potatoes with the remaining vegetables and spices; add
y mayonnaise. (Don't make the mayonnaise too thin; thicken it by adding
oil). Mix thoroughly. Season to taste. Chill and serve.

ATION

tute tahini dressing plus 2 tablespoons apple cider vinegar for soy
naise.

TOFU POTATO SALAD
Serves 4 to 6

potatoes, peeled and diced
ups water
reen peppers, diced
arrot, diced fine

2 medium onions, diced
3 stalks celery, diced
8 scallions, diced

potatoes in 4 cups of water over medium-high heat for 15 to 20 minutes,
il tender but not soft. Drain potatoes and place in a large bowl with
ning vegetables.

ing

-ounce cakes tofu
cup water
cup oil
easpoons sea salt

1 teaspoon ground dill seed
1 teaspoon caraway seed
1 teaspoon garlic powder
1/4 cup lemon juice

all ingredients in a blender until creamy smooth (if too thick add a
water; if too thin, add a little tofu). Pour over potatoes and vegetables.
for 4 to 6 hours. Stir often. Better the next day.

COLE SLAW #1
Serves 5

1 head of cabbage, shredded
2 stalks celery, chopped
4 carrots, grated
1 small onion, diced
2 peppers, diced
2 tablespoons tamari

2-1/2 cups so
(see recipe)
1 tablespoon a
1/2 teaspoon b
1/2 teaspoon p
1/2 teaspoon s

Place all the vegetables in a large bowl. Mix the mayonn
sonings, mixing well. Chill for 2 to 3 hours. Season to ta

COLE SLAW #2
Serves 6

Salad

1-1/2 heads cabbage, shredded
3 red peppers, diced

3 celery stalks
3 carrots, grat

Dressing

1/2 cup oil
1/3 cup apple cider vinegar
3 tablespoons tamari
1/2 cup tahini
1/3 cup water

1 teaspoon sea
1/2 teaspoon ga
1/2 teaspoon ba
1/2 teaspoon o1
1/2 teaspoon di

Combine all the salad items in a bowl. Place all the dre
a blender. Blend at high speed for 30 seconds. Pour th
vegetables and mix well. Chill and serve.
Best when allowed to sit, prepared, for 2 to 3 hours.

MACARONI SALAD
Serves 6

4 cups cooked whole wheat macaroni
2 green peppers, chopped
3 stalks celery, diced
1 onion, diced
1 garlic clove, minced
1/2 teaspoon sea salt
1/2 teaspoon basil

1/2 teaspoon pa
1/2 teaspoon o1
1/8 teaspoon re
1-1/2 cups tahi1
(see recipe)
2 tablespoons a
1 tablespoon blo

In a large bowl, combine all the ingredients except the dr
miso. Blend together remaining ingredients and pour o
Stir well; chill and serve.

10
3
4
3
2
1
2

Place
high
chill.
Co
the s
more

VAR

Subst
mayo

1
4
2
1

Cook
or u
rema

Dres

2
1
1
2

Blen
little
Chil

TOMATO TOFU SALAD
Serves 4 to 6

6 tomatoes, cut into chunks
1 8-ounce cake tofu, drained,
  pressed, and cut into chunks
1 onion, sliced
1 teaspoon sorghum

1/4 cup oil
3 tablespoons vinegar
1/2 teaspoon basil
1/4 teaspoon oregano

In a large bowl, combine the tomatoes, tofu, and onions. Blend together the oil, vinegar, and seasonings; add to the bowl, and allow to sit for up to 2 hours before serving.

COLD SWEET POTATO SALAD
Serves 5

7 sweet potatoes, baked or steamed
1 onion, diced
1 stalk celery, diced
2 tablespoons tamari

1/2 teaspoon garlic powder
1/2 teaspoon oregano
2 tablespoons tahini, (optional)

Peel and mash the sweet potatoes. Add the onion, celery, and seasonings. Add the tahini. Chill and serve with the salad course.

BULGHUR TABOULI SALAD
Serves 4

4 cups water
2 cups bulghur
1 head lettuce, shredded
1 cucumber, diced fine
2 tomatoes, diced fine
2 radishes, diced fine
3 scallions, diced fine

1/4 head cabbage, shredded
1/4 cup fresh parsley, chopped fine
3 tablespoons tamari
2 tablespoons oil
1/4 teaspoon garlic powder
1/4 teaspoon paprika
1/4 teaspoon basil

Place the water in a large saucepan over medium-high heat, and bring to a boil. Add the bulghur; add a pinch of salt if desired. Reduce heat to low; cover and simmer for approximately 15 to 20 minutes, or until the bulghur is soft and all the water is absorbed. Allow to cool.
 Combine all the vegetables in a large bowl. Add the bulghur and seasonings. Add dressing if desired.

VARIATION

Soak the bulghur in 4 cups water for an hour or more, until soft; drain and follow above recipe. Add other salad vegetables, such a beets, celery or peppers to the salad.
 Add 2 tablespoons of lemon juice or apple cider vinegar.

COLD BEAN SALAD
Serves 6

1 cup cooked pinto beans
1 cup cooked navy beans
1 cup cooked kidney beans
1 stalk celery, diced
1 green pepper, diced
2 garlic cloves, diced
2 onions, diced
1/2 cup oil
3 tablespoons tamari

2 tablespoons apple cider vinegar
1 tablespoon sorghum
3 tablespoons nutritional yeast
1/2 teaspoon sea salt
1/2 teaspoon garlic powder
1/4 teaspoon paprika
1/4 teaspoon oregano
1/4 teaspoon basil
1/8 teaspoon red pepper

Combine all the beans and diced vegetables in a large bowl. Place the remaining ingredients in a blender. Blend at high speed for 1 minute; then add to the bean and vegetable mixture, stirring well. Mix more liquid and add if desired. Chill for 2 hours to allow marination. Season to taste.

MASHED BEAN DIP
Serves 6

1 cup cooked lima beans
1 cup cooked pinto beans
1 cup cooked navy beans
1 onion, diced
1 stalk celery, diced
1 carrot, diced
1-1/2 cups tahini dressing (see recipe)

1/4 cup fresh parsley, diced
2 garlic cloves, minced
1/2 teaspoon garlic powder
1/4 teaspoon basil
1/4 teaspoon oregano
1/8 teaspoon red pepper

Combine the beans in a large bowl; mash well. Add the onion, celery, carrot, and tahini dressing. Mix in the spices. Chill and serve.

COLD CHICK-PEA SALAD
Serves 4 to 6

2 cups chick peas
5 cups water
1 onion, diced
1 stalk celery, diced
1/8 cup oil

1/3 cup tamari
1/2 teaspoon garlic powder
1/2 teaspoon cumin powder
1/4 teaspoon oregano
1/4 teaspoon sea salt

Place chick-peas and water in a pressure cooker and cook for 1-1/2 hours.
Or: Soak the chick-peas for 5 hours in enough water to cover, and drain water when ready to cook. Place them in a large pot with 5 cups water, and cook over medium heat for 2-1/2 hours, until soft.
Drain the chick-peas, reserving the stock for making dressings and soups. Mash the chick-peas; mix the oil in, add the remaining ingredients and mix well, till creamy. If dry, add some of the stock or a little more oil. Chill and serve.

VARIATION

Add diced vegetable saute to mixture.

COLD BROCCOLI SALAD
Serves 6

2 to 3 heads broccoli
1 sweet onion, diced
2 stalks celery, chopped
1/2 cup tahini

5 tablespoons tamari
1/2 teaspoon garlic powder
1/2 teaspoon paprika
1/4 teaspoon sea salt

Put the broccoli in a large saucepan with 4 cups water. Place over medium-high heat and steam for 15 minutes, or until tender. Drain the broccoli; place in a large bowl and mash until creamy smooth. Add the remaining ingredients, mixing well. Chill and serve.

VARIATION

Add chopped carrots and peppers with the other vegetables. Substitute cauliflower for the broccoli.

COLD CARROT SALAD
Serves 4 to 6

2 pounds carrots, peeled and sliced
1 large onion, chopped
2 stalks celery, chopped
1/2 cup tahini
1/4 teaspoon basil

5 tablespoons tamari
1-1/2 teaspoons lemon juice
1 teaspoon dill, seed or weed
1/4 teaspoon garlic powder
1/4 teaspoon oregano

Combine the carrots and 4 cups water in a large saucepan; place over medium-high heat and steam for 20 minutes or until soft. Drain off liquid. Transfer the carrots to a large bowl and mash well. Add the remaining ingredients and mix in. Chill and serve cold.

VARIATION

Saute 2 diced onions and 3 diced celery stalks, and add to the carrots.

EGGPLANT SALAD DIP
Serves 4 to 6

4 eggplants, peeled
1 onion, diced
4 garlic cloves, minced
5 tablespoons tahini

3 tablespoons tamari
1/2 teaspoon garlic powder
1/4 teaspoon basil
1/4 teaspoon sea salt

Chop the eggplants into large chunks. Place in a large saucepan with 3 cups water. Steam over medium-high heat for 15 minutes, until soft.

Drain the eggplant and transfer to a large bowl; mash well. Add the remaining ingredients. Chill and serve.

COLD STRING BEAN SALAD
Serves 4 to 6

2 pounds string beans
1 tablespoon oil
3 onions, diced
1-1/2 cups tahini dressing
(see recipe)

1/4 teaspoon garlic powder
1/4 teaspoon oregano
1/4 teaspoon paprika
1/4 teaspoon sea salt

Steam the string beans with 3 cups water in a large pot, for 20 minutes. Drain and mash. Heat the oil in a skillet, add the onions, saute for 7 minutes. In a bowl, combine the string beans, saute, and remaining ingredients. Chill and serve.

This may also be used as a dip.

VARIATION

Substitute raw onions for the sauteed ones.

PEPPERS-TOMATOES-POTATOES VINAIGRETTE
Serves 6

4 green or red sweet peppers,
sliced
2 small onions, sliced

3 tomatoes, diced
6 medium potatoes, cubed
2 cups water

Dressing:
1/4 cup oil
1/4 cup vinegar
1/4 cup water

1 teaspoon basil
1 teaspoon oregano
1 teaspoon garlic powder
2 tablespoons tamari

In a saucepan, steam potatoes in 2 cups of water until tender; drain and chill. Mix peppers, onions, and tomatoes in a bowl; add chilled potatoes. Blend all dressing ingredients in a blender for 1 minute; pour over vegetables, and let marinate for 2 to 3 hours.

VARIATION

Add 2 cups of lightly steamed cauliflower.

AVOCADO MARINADE
Serves 4

2 ripe avocados,
  peeled and cubed

1 onion, diced
1 tomato, cubed (optional)

Dressing:
1/4 cup oil
1/4 cup apple cider vinegar
1/2 cup water
2 teaspoons tamari

3 tablespoons nutritional yeast
2 tablespoons tahini
3 tablespoons chopped onion
1 clove fresh chopped garlic

Place cubed avocado, onion, and tomato in a bowl. Blend all dressing ingredients in a blender until creamy smooth. Pour into bowl, chill and let marinate for 1 hour before serving.

VARIATION

Add 1 cup of cubed tofu.

"I will not kill or hurt any living creature need-
lessly, nor destroy any beautiful thing, but will
strive to save and comfort all gentle life, and
guard and protect all natural beauty upon the
earth...."

"Do not fancy that you will lower yourselves by
sympathy with the lower creatures; you cannot
sympathize rightly with the higher, unless you do
with those."

John Ruskin

"It often happens that the universal belief of one age, a belief from which no one was free or could be free without an extraordinary effort of genius or courage, becomes to a subsequent age, so palpable an absurdity that the only difficulty is, to imagine how such an idea could ever have appeared credible."

John Stuart Mill

"We manage to swallow flesh, only because we do not think of the cruel and sinful thing we do. There are many crimes which are the creation of man himself, the wrongfullness of which is put down to their divergence from habit, custom, or tradition. But cruelty is not of these. It is a fundamental sin, and admits of no arguments or nice distinctions. If only we do not allow our heart to grow callous, it protests against cruelty, is always clearly heard; and yet we go on perpetrating cruelties easily, merrily, all of us— in fact, anyone who does not join in is dubbed a crank. ....if, after our pity is aroused, we persist in throttling our feelings simply in order to join others in preying upon life, we insult all that is good in us. I have decided to try a vegetarian diet."

Rabindranath Tagore

Dressings and Sauces

BEET DRESSING
Serves 4 to 6

1 beet, steamed and grated
1 cup water
1/4 cup oil
3 tablespoons vinegar
2 tablespoons tamari
3 tablespoons tahini

1/2 teaspoon sea salt
1/4 teaspoon basil
1/4 teaspoon oregano
1 teaspoon sorghum
Handful of chives
    or 1 scallion, chopped

Place all the ingredients in a blender; blend at medium speed for 45 seconds. Season to taste.

ITALIAN OLIVE OIL DRESSING
Serves 4 to 6

1/4 cup olive oil
1/4 cup water
4 tablespoons lime or lemon juice
3 tablespoons apple cider vinegar
2 tablespoons tamari

4 garlic cloves, diced
2 tablespoons onion, chopped
1 teaspoon oregano
1/2 teaspoon basil
1/2 teaspoon garlic powder

In a medium size jar, combine all the ingredients; shake well. Refrigerate for 2 to 3 days before serving.

TAHINI DRESSING
Serves 4 to 6

1/2 cup tahini
2/3 cup water
2 tablespoons tamari
1/8 teaspoon garlic powder

1/3 teaspoon paprika
1/8 teaspoon basil
1/8 teaspoon oregano
1/4 small onion, diced

Place all of the ingredients in a blender; blend for 1 minute, until creamy.

HOUSE DRESSING
Serves 6 to 8

1/2 cup oil
1/4 apple cider vinegar
1/3 cup tamari
1 cup tahini
1 teaspoon sorghum

1-1/2 cups water or vegetable stock
1/2 teaspoon garlic powder
1/2 teaspoon sea salt
1/2 teaspoon paprika
1/4 teaspoon sweet basil

Combine the water and tahini in a blender and blend at medium speed for 30 seconds. Add the remaining ingredients and blend until smooth and creamy.
    For a thinner dressing, add more stock; for a thicker dressing add more tahini.

GARDEN TAHINI DRESSING
Serves 4 to 6

5 tablespoons tahini
1 tablespoon lemon juice
1 cup water
1/4 onion, diced
2 tablespoons tamari

1 garlic clove, minced
3 tablespoons oil
1 comfrey leaf
1/2 cup raw salad vegetables

Place all of the ingredients in a blender; blend at medium speed for a minute until creamy smooth. Season to taste.

TOFU TAHINI DRESSING
Serves 4 to 6

1 cup water
1 8-ounce cake tofu
1/4 cup tahini
1/4 teaspoon caraway seeds
1/4 teaspoon dill weed

1/4 teaspoon garlic powder
2 garlic cloves, diced
2 tablespoons onion, diced
3 tablespoons lime or lemon juice
2 tablespoons tamari

Combine all the ingredients in a blender; blend at high speed for a minute until smooth. Add more liquid (water or stock) if needed. Chill and serve.

BLOND MISO DRESSING
Serves 4

1 cup water
1/4 cup oil
1/8 cup apple cider vinegar
2 tablespoons sorghum
1/4 onion, diced

3 tablespoons blond miso
1 tablespoon nut butter
1/4 teaspoon garlic powder
1/4 teaspoon paprika

Combine all ingredients in a blender; blend at medium speed for a minute until creamy. To make thinner, add more liquid; to make thicker, add more nut butter.

ZUCCHINI DRESSING
Serves 4

1/2 cup oil
1 medium sized zucchini, diced
1 small onion, diced
1/2 cup water
2 tablespoons tamari

1 teaspoon vinegar
1/8 teaspoon garlic powder
1/8 teaspoon basil
1/8 teaspoon sea salt
1/8 teaspoon parsley

Combine all the ingredients in a blender; blend at high speed for a minute. Season to taste. Chill and serve.

ORANGE TAMARI DRESSING
Serves 4 to 6

1 cup oil
1/2 cup orange juice
1/4 cup tamari
1/8 cup apple cider vinegar
1/4 teaspoon garlic powder

1/8 teaspoon sea salt
1/8 teaspoon celery salt
1/8 teaspoon paprika
1 tablespoon sorghum (optional)

Combine all the ingredients in a blender; blend at medium speed. Add the sorghum for a sweeter dressing, if desired.

VEGAN FRENCH DRESSING
Serves 4 to 6

1-1/2 cups stewed,
   or soft uncooked, tomatoes
1/2 cup tahini
1/8 cup tamari
1/4 teaspoon oregano

1/4 teaspoon garlic powder
1/4 teaspoon parsley
1/4 teaspoon sea salt
1/4 teaspoon basil

Place the tomatoes in a blender; blend at medium speed for a minute until almost a liquid. Add the tahini, tamari, and seasonings; then reblend.
  If too thick, add more tomatoes or 1/2 cup vegetable stock.

SOY MAYONNAISE
Yields 1-1/2 cups

1/2 cup soy milk (see recipe)
2 tablespoons vinegar or lemon juice
1/4 teaspoon garlic powder

1/4 teaspoon paprika
1/4 teaspoon sea salt
1 cup oil

Place all ingredients except the oil in a blender. Blend at high speed for a minute, adding the oil gradually while blender is running.

HUMMUS SAUCE
Serves 4 to 6

1 cup cooked chick peas
1/2 cup tahini
2-1/2 cups water
2 teaspoons cumin powder

1 tablespoon lemon juice
1-1/2 teaspoons sea salt
1 teaspoon paprika
2 garlic cloves, diced

Combine all the ingredients in a blender; blend at high speed for a minute. Season to taste. This sauce is great on falafel or any salad.

COMFREY DRESSING
Yields 3-1/2 to 4 cups

1 cup oil
2 cups vegetable stock
1/4 cup lemon juice
3 comfrey leaves, chopped
3 garlic cloves, diced
1/2 medium onion, diced

4 tablespoons tahini or peanut butter
2 tablespoons tamari
1/2 teaspoon sea salt
1/2 teaspoon garlic powder
1/2 teaspoon oregano
1/2 teaspoon parsley

Combine all the ingredients in a blender; blend at medium speed for 30 seconds until smooth.

SPICY DIP
Yields 1-1/2 cups

2 tablespoons oil
1 tablespoon water
1 8-ounce cake tofu

1/2 teaspoon garlic powder
1/2 small onion, grated

In a blender, combine all the ingredients except the onion. Blend at high speed for a minute, until the tofu is creamy; place mixture in a bowl and add the grated onion.
Delicious with crackers, bread, or salad.

GARLIC OIL SPREAD

1/4 cup oil
2 garlic cloves, diced

1 tablespoon tahini
1/4 teaspoon salt

Combine all the ingredients in a blender and blend at high speed for a minute. Serve as a sauce or spread.

MISO SPREAD
Yields 8 ounces

3 tablespoons miso
1 tablespoon tahini
1 tablespoon sesame meal
1 scallion, chopped

1 tablespoon oil
1 teaspoon sweetener
1/4 teaspoon basil

In a bowl, combine all the ingredients, mixing well. Delicious on whole wheat bread with tomato and sprouts.

SUNFLOWER SPREAD
Yields 1 cup

1/2 cup sunflower seeds   1 teaspoon sweetener (optional)
1/2 cup water

Place ingredients in blender. Blend at medium speed for a minute until thick and creamy.
Good for breakfast spread, sandwiches, or with fruit.

VARIATION

Substitute other seeds and nuts for the sunflower seeds.

WARM AVOCADO SAUCE
Yields 2 cups

4 ripe avocados   1/4 teaspoon oregano
1 tablespoon oil   1/4 teaspoon basil
1 onion, diced   1/4 teaspoon garlic powder
3 tablespoons tamari   1/4 teaspoon sea salt

Scoop avocados out of shell, and mash them in a bowl. Heat the oil in a large frying pan over medium heat; add the remaining ingredients, except the avocado, and saute until tender. Add the avocado; reduce heat and cook until warm, stirring constantly.
This sauce does not keep well; make only enough for one meal. Delicious over vegetables and grains.

BEAN SAUCE
Yields 2 cups

1 cup cooked beans   1/2 teaspoon oregano
  (kidney, pinto, lima, etc.)   1/2 teaspoon basil
1/2 cup water or stock   1/2 teaspoon paprika
3 tablespoons tamari   1/8 teaspoon red pepper
1 teaspoon garlic powder

Put the beans and water in a blender; blend at high speed for a minute until creamy, adding more liquid if needed.
Add the remaining ingredients. Pour into a saucepan, warm over medium heat, and serve.

SESAME MEAL
Yields 1 cup

1 cup sesame seeds   1/2 teaspoon sea salt

Place 2 tablespoons of the sesame seeds in a blender and blend well. Add the remaining seeds by 2 tablespoon measurements, blending well after each addition. Mix in the salt.

Use as a dressing on salads, casseroles, and broiled vegetables, or as a condiment.

CHEESY GRAVY
Yields 2 cups

1/2 cup nutritional yeast   1/2 teaspoon garlic powder
1/3 cup flour   1/4 teaspoon paprika
1/4 cup oil   1/4 teaspoon basil
1 to 2 cups stock or water   1/4 teaspoon oregano
1-1/2 tablespoons tamari

In a medium saucepan, combine the yeast and flour; place over a low heat, stirring until lightly toasted. Add the oil, stirring to make a thick batter. Slowly add the stock, stirring constantly (add liquid until desired consistency is reached).

Add the remaining ingredients, and stir well. Serve over vegetables.

CHEESY GRAVY QUICK METHOD

1/2 cup tahini   1-1/2 to 2 cups water
1/2 cup nutritional yeast   or vegetable stock
1/8 cup tamari

Place all ingredients in blender, blend at medium speed for 30 seconds, until creamy. Season to taste with sea salt, garlic powder.

NUTRITIONAL YEAST GRAVY
Yields 2-1/2 cups

1-1/2 cups stock or water   3 tablespoons tamari
1/2 cup nutritional yeast   1/2 teaspoon garlic powder
1/4 cup tahini   1/2 teaspoon basil
1/8 onion, diced   1/2 teaspoon oregano
1 garlic clove, diced   1/2 teaspoon sea salt

Combine the stock, nutritional yeast and tahini in a blender; blend at medium speed for a minute. Add the remaining ingredients; blend well at high speed. Add more liquid to thin, or tahini to thicken. Season to taste.

Pour gravy into medium sized saucepan; place over low heat and cook until warmed, stirring constantly.

CORN MEAL/YEAST GRAVY
Yields 4 cups

3 cups water
1/2 cup cornmeal
2 tablespoons tamari
1 onion, diced
2 scallions, diced
2 tablespoons tahini or peanut butter

1/2 cup nutritional yeast
1/2 teaspoon garlic powder
1/2 teaspoon basil
1/2 teaspoon oregano
1/2 teaspoon sea salt

Place the water in a medium sized saucepan; bring to a slow boil over medium heat. Add the cornmeal, tamari, and seasonings, stirring well; add onion, scallions, and nut butter. Cook the mixture for 5 minutes. Add nutritional yeast and stir well.

If gravy is too thick, add more water. For a creamier consistency, blend gravy for 30 seconds and reheat.

CHEESE TOPPING
Yields 4 cups

2 cups nutritional yeast
6 tablespoons arrowroot powder
1/4 teaspoon paprika
2/3 cup whole wheat flour
2 cups water

1 tablespoon oil
1/2 teaspoon garlic powder
Dash of pepper
1/2 cup soy margarine
   (see recipe)

Mix dry ingredients in a medium sized pot. Gradually add the water and oil; making a smooth paste. Thin with remaining water. Place on medium heat, stirring constantly, until it thickens and bubbles. Add garlic powder and pepper. Remove from heat and whip in margarine. Let cool. Serve as topping for any vegetable.

CREAMY SAUCE
Yields 2 cups

2 tablespoons whole wheat flour
1/2 tablespoon oil

1/4 cup tamari
1 cup water or stock

Combine the flour and oil in a small bowl; spread over the bottom of a small saucepan and toast over medium heat until golden brown, stirring constantly. Place pan in the refrigerator to cool.

When cool, add the water, mixing well; place over low heat, stirring constantly, until desired consistency is reached. For thicker sauce, add a little more flour.

Delicious over steamed vegetables and grains.

CREAMY GARLIC SAUCE
Yields 3 cups

2 tablespoons tahini
1-1/2 cups water
1/3 cup nutritional yeast
2 tablespoons arrowroot powder

3 garlic cloves, minced
3 scallions, diced
1/2 teaspoon garlic powder
1/2 teaspoon celery salt

Combine the tahini and water in a medium sized saucepan; add the nutritional yeast. Sift the arrowroot powder (sift through a strainer), and add to the mixture; add the remaining ingredients, mixing well after each addition.

Place pan over low heat, cook for approximately 5 minutes, stirring often, until sauce is thick.

HOT MISO DRESSING
Yields 3 cups

2 tablespoons whole wheat flour
2 tablespoons oil
2-1/2 cups stock or water
1 small onion, diced
3 scallion tops, diced

4 tablespoons miso paste
  and 1/2 cup water
1/2 teaspoon garlic powder
1 tablespoon sorghum (optional)

Combine the flour and oil in a medium sized saucepan; place over medium heat and toast for 3 minutes until golden brown, stirring constantly. Add the stock, onion and scallions and stir well.

When mixture boils, reduce heat; dilute the miso with the water and add to saucepan. Add the garlic powder and continue stirring until a creamy consistency is reached. For a sweet and spicy taste, add the sorghum.

MUSHROOM SAUCE
Yields 1 quart

1/2 cup flour
1/2 cup oil
3 cloves garlic, diced
3 onions, diced
1 green pepper, diced
1 stalk celery, diced

1/2 pound mushrooms, sliced
3 cups vegetable stock or water
1/4 cup tamari
1 teaspoon parsley
1 teaspoon garlic powder
1/2 teaspoon sea salt

In a medium sized saucepan, over medium heat, stir in the flour and 1/4 cup of oil. Quick fry until golden brown. Put this mixture aside; using the same saucepan, add the remaining 1/4 cup oil, garlic, onions, celery, and pepper, and saute for 7 minutes. Add the mushrooms and cook 3 minutes more.

Place the stock and the flour mixture in a blender; blend at medium speed for 30 seconds until homogenized. Add blended mixture to saute. Season with tamari, parsley, garlic powder, and sea salt. Cook on low heat for 10 minutes. For a thicker sauce, add more flour.

SPRING GREENS PUREE
Serves 5 or 6

1 pound fresh greens
   (spinach, chard or kale)
2 tablespoons oil
Sea salt to taste

1 garlic clove, crushed
2 tablespoons tahini
   or thick soy milk

Wash and drain the greens; cut into small pieces. Combine in a large sauce-pan with the oil and garlic. Place over medium heat and cook for 5 minutes, or until tender, stirring often. Transfer the greens to a blender. Add the tahini or soy milk and blend at medium speed for one minute, until smooth. Season to taste. Reheat and serve garnished, with steamed or baked vege-tables.

VARIATION

For a creamier sauce, remove the stems from greens and steam before blending.

STANDARD GRAVY
(Yields 1-1/2 cups)

1/2 cup whole wheat flour
2 tablespoons oil
1 cup water or stock
2 tablespoons tahini

2 tablespoons tamari
1/2 teaspoon garlic powder
1/4 teaspoon celery seeds

Combine the flour and oil in a small saucepan; place over low heat and toast until brown, stirring constantly. Add enough of the water or stock to reach desired consistency; add the tahini and remaining ingredients, mixing well after each addition. Simmer for at least 20 minutes, stirring often.

For a creamier gravy, blend at medium speed for 30 seconds. Reheat.

SWEET AND SOUR SAUCE
Yields 3-1/2 cups

3 tablespoons whole wheat flour
2 tablespoons oil
3 cups vegetable stock
   (preferably carrot or pumpkin)
1 tablespoon arrowroot powder

1 teaspoon sorghum
3 scallion tops, diced
2 tablespoons tamari
1 teaspoon vinegar
1 teaspoon garlic powder

In a large saucepan, combine the flour and oil; place over medium heat and toast for 3 minutes until light brown, stirring constantly to prevent burning. Allow to cool. Add the vegetable stock; sift the arrowroot powder, and add to the sauce.

Mix in the remaining ingredients, stirring well. Place over low heat and cook for 5 minutes. For a thinner sauce, add a little more stock; to thicken, add a little flour. For creamier sauce blend at medium speed for 30 seconds.

TAHINI-TAMARI SAUCE
Yields 4 cups

1 tablespoon oil
2 garlic cloves, minced
1 large onion, diced
1-1/2 cups tahini
2-1/2 cups water

1/3 cup tamari
1/4 teaspoon basil
1/4 teaspoon oregano
1/4 teaspoon garlic powder

In a saucepan, heat the oil over medium heat; add the garlic and onion, and saute for 5 minutes.

Combine the tahini, water, and tamari in a blender; blend at medium speed for 30 seconds. Add this mixture to the saute; add seasonings if desired. Reduce heat and cook for 5 minutes. To thicken, add more tahini.

TOMATO SAUCE
Yields 3 quarts

7 pounds ripe tomatoes
1/2 cup flour, sifted
1/4 cup oil
6 garlic cloves, diced
3 celery stalks, diced
3 large onions, diced
2 green peppers, diced
1 carrot, diced
2 bay leaves

1 tablespoon garlic powder
1 tablespoon basil
1 tablespoon oregano
1 tablespoon parsley
1 teaspoon sea salt
1/2 teaspoon marjoram
2 tablespoons sorghum
3 tablespoons arrowroot powder

Cut the tomatoes into quarters and place in a large pot with 1/2'' of water. Cook over low heat for approximately 15 minutes, until soft. Add the flour. Pour the tomatoes into a blender, and blend at medium speed for 1 minute. Return mixture to the pot.

In a large frying pan, heat the oil over medium-high heat; add 2 cloves of the garlic, the celery, onions, peppers, and carrot, and saute for 7 minutes, until tender. Pour the sauteed vegetables into a blender, blend at medium speed for a minute; add to the blended tomato mixture. Add the bay leaves and half of the seasoning. Cook over low heat for 3 to 4 hours, stirring occasionally.

Add the 4 remaining garlic cloves, the remaining seasonings, and the sorghum. Cook for 1-1/2 hours longer. For a thicker sauce, add 3 tablespoons of arrowroot powder (sifted through a strainer) and stir well; cook for 5 minutes longer. This sauce can be frozen and stored.

VARIATION

Add 1 cup diced mushrooms with the remaining garlic and seasonings.

QUICK TOMATO SAUCE
Yields 1-1/2 quarts

2 tablespoons oil
4 garlic cloves, diced
2 large onions, diced
1 stalk celery, diced
2 peppers, diced
4 tablespoons tamari
1 teaspoon sea salt

1 teapoon oregano
1 teaspoon garlic powder
1 teaspoon paprika
12 ripe tomatoes
2 tablespoons sorghum
2 tablespoons arrowroot powder

Heat the oil in a large soup pot; add the garlic, onions, celery, peppers, and seasonings, and saute for about 7 minutes.

Put in a blender: the tomatoes, sorghum, and arrowroot powder; blend at medium speed for 1 minute. It will take 2 blender batches to do it all.

Add blended mixture to soup pot. Cook for 1 hour, uncovered. For a creamier sauce, re-blend.

VEGAN SALTEADO
Yields 5 cups

4 cups tomato sauce (see recipe)
1/4 cup olive oil
1 small onion, diced
1 cup green peas

1 8-ounce cake tofu, diced
1 bay leaf
1/2 teaspoon garlic powder
1/4 teaspoon basil

Combine all the ingredients in a large pot. Cook over low heat for approximately 30 minutes, until soupy. Serve over potatoes.

CARROT SAUCE
Yields 3 cups

4 carrots, cut into chunks
1 onion, cut into chunks
2 garlic cloves, minced
3 tablespoons oil
1 to 1-1/2 cups stock or water

1 tablespoon tamari
2 tablespoons tahini
  or peanut butter
1/2 teaspoon sea salt
1/2 teaspoon garlic powder

In a medium sized pot, steam carrots and onion in 2 cups water, for 15 minutes. Drain liquid. In a blender, place the steamed vegetables and add the remaining ingredients. Blend at medium speed for 30 seconds until creamy, adding liquid to thin, or more carrots to thicken. Cook for 5 to 7 minutes on low heat.

Serve hot over grains or vegetables, or as a dip for dinner rolls.

CHINESE SAUCE
Yields 4 to 5 cups

1/3 cup oil
10 garlic cloves, chopped
1/2 teaspoon fresh ginger, diced
1/2 cup sorghum

3-1/2 cups stock
4 tablespoons arrowroot powder
1/3 cup tamari sauce

In a saucepan, heat oil over medium high heat until it is hot. Add the garlic and ginger and boil in oil until browned. Let cool for 10 minutes.

In a blender, combine the remaining ingredients and cooked oil mixture. Blend at medium speed till smooth— about 30 seconds. Return to saucepan and simmer on low heat until thick (about 15 to 20 minutes).

"The sad and serious state of our planet demands a newer age, in which that holy word "Love" is lived upon heights never known by the human race; a truly loving age, safe for human beings and for all who live."

"First and foremost, violence and cruelty must be abolished. Compassion, the essence of love, needs to become a spiritual standard and a living ethic."

"The Vegan Evolution will inspire a heightened spiritual awareness, purify the body, and make possible personal and planetary healing unprecedented in human history."

Sun
"A Newer Age"

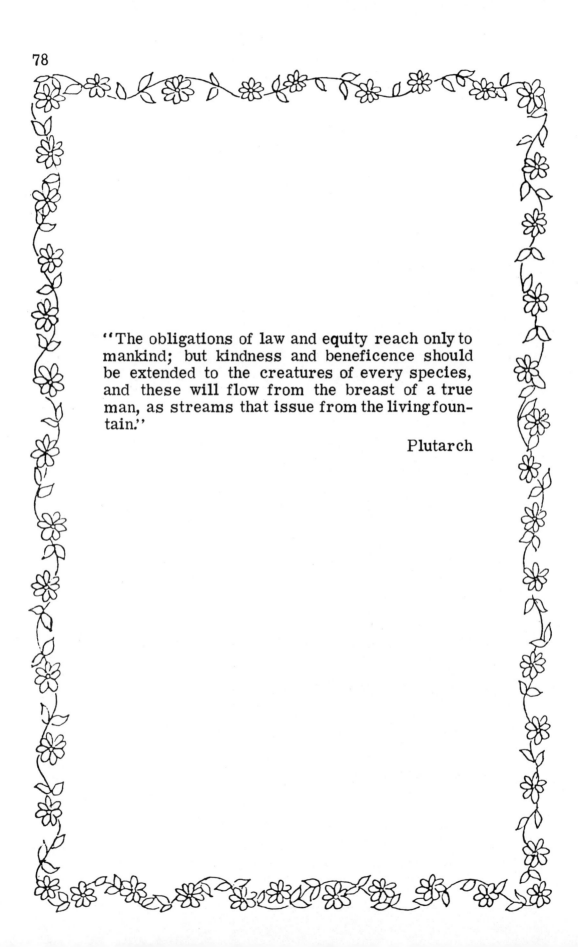

"The obligations of law and equity reach only to mankind; but kindness and beneficence should be extended to the creatures of every species, and these will flow from the breast of a true man, as streams that issue from the living fountain."

Plutarch

" 'Thou shalt not kill' does not apply to murder of one's own kind only, but to all living beings; and this Commandment was inscribed in the human breast long before it was proclaimed from Sinai."

Count Leo Tolstoy

"If a man's aspirations towards a righteous life are serious.... if he earnestly seeks a righteous life, his first act of abstinence is from animal food, because, not to mention the excitement of the passions produced by such food, it is plainly immoral, as it requires an act contrary to moral feeling, i.e., killing-and is called forth only by greed."

Count Leo Tolstoy

Count Tolstoy had invited to dinner a non-vegetarian lady, who had stipulated that meat must be served. As he escorted her to the dinner table, she found a live chicken tied to her chair. When asked the meaning of this, the great man replied, "My conscience forbids me to kill it; as you are the only guest taking meat I would be greatly obliged if you would undertake the killing first." It is reported that the meal was strictly vegetarian!

Side Dishes

Beginner Recipes

GARDEN STEAM
Serves 6

4 zucchini, cut into chunks
2 cups fresh peas
1/2 head cabbage, cut into chunks
2 carrots, cut into chunks

4 beets, cut into chunks
1/2 head cauliflower,
  cut into chunks
1/2 head broccoli, cut into chunks

In a large stainless steel pot, place 2 cups of water and a steamer; add all the vegetables, placing the firmer ones (such as the beets and carrots) on the bottom. Steam over medium heat for 12 minutes, until lightly tender.

STEAMED GREENS
Serves 4

1-1/2 cups water
1 pound greens
  (fresh cabbage, Swiss chard,
  beet tops, kale or spinach)

1 onion, sliced
2 teaspoons tamari
2 teaspoons oil
1/2 teaspoon fresh garlic, minced

Place the water in a medium sized pot with a steamer inside. Water should be about 2 inches deep. Cut the greens into bite-size pieces and add to the pot. Top with the remaining ingredients.

Cook over medium-high heat for 10 minutes, till the greens are soft. The Swiss chard, beet tops, and spinach cook quicker than the other items; collards take longer, about 20 minutes.

Serve with lemon or lime wedges.

BAKED BEETS
Serves 4

6 beets
1/4 cup oil
3 tablespoons tamari

1/4 teaspoon garlic powder
1/4 teaspoon oregano
1/4 teaspoon sea salt

Preheat oven to 375 F. Scrub the beets and puncture several times with a fork. Combine oil, tamari and spices in a bowl; brush this mixture on the beets. Place on a baking sheet and bake for approximately 1 hour, until soft.

To shorten baking time, slice the beets before baking.

SLICED BUTTERNUT
Serves 4 to 6

2 butternut squash
1/4 cup oil
3 tablespoons tamari

2 tablespoons water
1/2 teaspoon garlic powder

Preheat oven to 375 F. Scrub the squash well and cut in half lengthwise; scoop the seeds out. Cut into long, 1-inch wide slices. Place on a baking sheet.

Combine the remaining ingredients and brush on the squash slices. Bake for 45 minutes or until tender.

BAKED CARROTS AND ONIONS
Serves 4

5 large carrots, peeled
3 to 6 small onions, peeled

1/4 teaspoon sea salt

Preheat oven to 375 F. Place the carrots and onions in a baking dish; add 1-1/2 inches of water and sprinkle with salt. Cover and bake for 30 to 45 minutes.

VARIATION

Substitute whole beets for the carrots or onions.

BAKED FRESH CORN
Serves 4

8 unhusked ears of corn

Preheat oven to 350 F. Bake the corn for approximately 15 minutes, until the husks are golden brown.
OR:
Place the corn in a casserole dish; add 1/2-inch of water, cover and bake for approximately 15 minutes.

BAKED PEPPERS AND ONIONS
Serves 4

6 medium green peppers, sliced
2 medium onions, sliced
2 tablespoons tamari

1/2 teaspoon garlic powder
1/4 teaspoon paprika

Preheat oven to 350 F. Oil a baking sheet. Place the peppers and onions on the baking sheet. Season with tamari and garlic powder; sprinkle with paprika.
Bake for 30 minutes, or until tender, and the onions are golden brown.

SLICE' EM AND BAKE' EM POTATOES
Serves 4 to 6

5 to 8 potatoes	1/4 teaspoon sea salt
1/3 cup oil	1/4 teaspoon paprika
2 tablespoons tamari	1/4 teaspoon garlic powder

Preheat oven to 350 F. Scrub the unpeeled potatoes well. Slice lengthwise into thin strips, or cut into chunks. Combine the remaining ingredients. Add a squirt of lemon juice, if desired.

Place the potatoes on a baking sheet; brush with the mixture. Or, first place the potatoes in the bowl with the mixture, and then scoop onto the baking sheet.

Bake for 30 minutes, or until golden brown, turning over every 10 to 15 minutes.

VARIATION

Add 2 sliced onions with the potatoes.

BAKED SPAGHETTI SQUASH
Serves 2

1 large spaghetti squash	1/2 cup tahini dressing;
	or cheesy gravy;
	or tomato sauce;
	or tamari, oil, garlic mix
	(see recipes)

Preheat oven to 350 F. Cut the squash in half and scoop out the seeds; place on a baking sheet, cut side up. Bake for 30 to 40 minutes, or until tender. Lightly separate the squash from its skin with a fork to make spaghetti-like strands. Pour the sauce over both halves. Bake for 5 minutes more.

BAKED SQUASH ON THE HALF SHELL
Serves 6 to 8

3 large zucchini	1 teaspoon garlic powder
1/4 cup oil	1/2 small onion, diced
2 tablespoons miso, or	1 garlic clove, diced
1/4 cup tamari	1/4 teaspoon paprika
3 tablespoons nutritional yeast	

Preheat oven to 350 F. Cut zucchini in half lengthwise. Place in baking dish, cut side face up. Slash 3 or 4 times lengthwise so dressing will soak into the squash.

Blend remaining ingredients at high speed for 30 seconds. Pour a little over each squash and spread out. Bake for 10 minutes with a little water in dish, and cover; baste again with dressing. Remove cover. Sprinkle with paprika and bake 15 minutes more. Place under broiler for 2 minutes to brown.

BAKED ZUCCHINI
Serves 4

8 small or medium zucchini
(garden fresh are best)

Preheat oven to 350 F. Rinse the zucchini; place in a large baking dish with 1/4-inch of water. Do not cut off the tips of the squash or liquid will drain out. Bake for 30 minutes covered, or until tender.

VARIATION

Slice a center wedge out of the length of the zucchini, remove and stuff with a mix of minced garlic and oil. Bake as above.

BROILED SQUASH
Serves 4

5 large zucchini, crookneck, or
   white scalloped squash
1/3 cup oil
3 tablespoons tamari
2 tablespoons water

1/2 teaspoon garlic powder
1/2 teaspoon paprika
1/4 teaspoon sea salt
1 teaspoon lemon juice (optional)

Preheat oven to broil. Slice the squash into long strips, 1/4-inch thick. Combine remaining ingredients in a bowl. Place the slices of squash, side by side, on a baking sheet, and brush top with the dressing mixture. Broil for 4 or 5 minutes until brown, watching closely to prevent burning.

BROILED TOMATOES
Serves 4 to 6

6 firm, red tomatoes
1/4 cup oil
1/4 cup tamari
1/4 cup water
3 tablespoons sesame seeds
4 tablespoons wheat germ

2 tablespoons bran
1/2 teaspoon garlic powder
1/4 teaspoon basil
1/4 teaspoon oregano
1/4 teaspoon sea salt

Preheat oven to broil. Slice the tomatoes into 1/4-inch rounds; place on a baking sheet. Sprinkle lightly with sea salt. Combine the remaining ingredients to make a thick paste. Place a spoonful on top of each tomato; press down to flatten, like breading.

Broil or bake for 5 to 7 minutes, until breading is golden brown.

CREAM CORN
Serves 4

5 cups corn kernels
2 cups tahini dressing (see recipe)
1 8-ounce cake tofu
5 tablespoons nutritional yeast
3 garlic cloves, diced

1 small onion, diced
1 tablespoon sorghum
1/2 teaspoon garlic powder
1/4 teaspoon paprika
1/4 teaspoon sea salt

In a medium sized saucepan, combine the corn kernels and tahini dressing; blend in the tofu. Add the remaining ingredients. Cook over medium heat for approximately 20 minutes. Season to taste.

CREAMED SPINACH
Serves 3 to 4

2 pounds spinach   1 cup cheesy gravy (see recipe)

Place the spinach in a large pot with 2 inches of water; steam over medium heat for 5 minutes, until tender. Drain; add the sauce and mix well.

If desired, place 1/2 cup of the mixture in a blender and blend for 30 seconds; return to remaining spinach and serve.

VARIATION

Can substitute Swiss chard for the spinach.

HOME FRIED POTATOES
Serves 4 to 6

2 tablespoons oil
3 garlic cloves, diced
2 onions, sliced
8 large baked potatoes,
   peeled and sliced
3 stalks celery, chopped

2 green peppers, diced
1/2 pound mushrooms,
   cut into chunks
2 to 3 tablespoons tamari
1/2 teaspoon garlic powder
1/2 teaspoon oregano

Heat the oil in a large skillet over medium-high heat; add 2 cloves of the garlic, onions, potatoes, celery, and peppers; saute for 5 minutes. Add the mushrooms and saute for 3 minutes more. Mix in the remaining garlic and the seasonings, adjusting to taste. Simmer on low heat for 3 minutes.

Add a creamy sauce such as standard gravy (see recipe), and cook for 3 minutes more.

VARIATION

Use steamed potatoes instead of baked; or raw potatoes and add to the saute first.

HASH BROWNS
Serves 4 to 6

5 medium potatoes	2 tablespoons nutritional yeast
2 tablespoons oil	2 tablespoons tamari
2 Spanish onions, chopped	1 teaspoon kelp

Preheat oven to 350 F. Bake the potatoes for 30 minutes. When cool, cut into 1/2-inch slices.

Heat the oil in a skillet over medium heat; add the onions and potatoes, and saute for 10 minutes, until tender. Add the nutritional yeast, tamari, and kelp, while pan is still over the heat. Season to taste.

POTATO OREGANO
Serves 4 to 6

3 tablespoons oil	1-1/2 teaspoons oregano
5 garlic cloves, diced	1 teaspoon sea salt
3 large onions, diced	1 teaspoon basil
3 green peppers, diced	1/2 teaspoon garlic powder
8 potatoes, steamed and	2 tomatoes, cut into chunks
cut into chunks	(optional)
2 tablespoons tamari	

Heat the oil in a large skillet, over medium-high heat. Add the garlic, onions, and peppers, and saute for 5 minutes. Add the steamed potatoes and the seasonings, stirring often. Add the tomatoes; season to taste. Cook for 3 minutes more. Also delicious served the next day.

MASHED POTATOES
Serves 4

5 large potatoes, cut into chunks	1 teaspoon garlic powder
2 tablespoons oil	1 teaspoon basil
2 garlic cloves, diced	1/2 teaspoon sea salt
1 green pepper, diced	1/2 teaspoon paprika
2 stalks celery, diced	1/2 cup tahini dressing
3 tablespoons tamari	(see recipe)

In a large pot or pressure cooker, combine the potatoes with 2 cups water; boil over medium heat for 15 minutes (5 minutes in a pressure cooker), adding a peeled and sliced onion or 2 sliced carrots to the pot for flavor, if desired.

In a skillet, heat the oil over medium-high heat; add the garlic and onions and saute for 5 minutes. Add the remaining vegetables and saute for 5 minutes more, adding the seasonings while cooking.

Drain the potatoes and mash well. Combine with the sauteed vegetables, mixing well. Whip the tahini dressing into the potatoes, using a fork, until a smooth consistency is reached.

VEGETABLE SPAGHETTI SQUASH ITALIANO
Serves 4 to 6

2 spaghetti squash
2 tablespoons oil
3 garlic cloves, diced
2 onions, diced
2 celery stalks, diced

1 pepper, diced
1 teaspoon basil
1 teaspoon oregano
1 tablespoon garlic powder
2 cups tomato sauce (see recipe)

In a large pot, combine the whole spaghetti squash with 5 cups water; boil over medium heat for 35 to 45 minutes, till easily punctured with a fork. Remove from pot, cut in half, scoop out the seeds using a fork, gently scoop out the spaghetti squash strands, placing them in a large bowl.

In a frying pan, heat the oil over medium-high heat; add the garlic, onions, celery, pepper and seasonings, and saute for 7 minutes, until vegetables are tender. Add to the squash. Mix in the sauce, and serve.

ONION SAUTE
Serves 4

2 tablespoons oil
3 garlic cloves, diced
2 large onions, sliced
2 tablespoons tamari
5 outer lettuce leaves, shredded

2 teaspoons arrowroot powder
1/2 teaspoon garlic powder
1/2 teaspoon basil
1/4 teaspoon oregano

In a skillet, heat the oil over medium-high heat; add the garlic, and saute for 2 minutes, until golden. Add the onions and tamari, and cook for 5 minutes, until the onions are almost soft. Add the lettuce.

Sift the arrowroot powder into the saute and stir well for approximately 2 minutes until the liquid begins to thicken. Mix in the spices and cook for 1 minute more.

SAUTEED SPINACH
Serves 4 to 6

2 tablespoons oil
4 large onions, sliced
2 stalks celery, chopped
2 peppers, sliced
1/2 pound mushrooms,
  cut into chunks
1-1/2 pounds fresh spinach

1/2 head cabbage,
  cut into large chunks
1/4 teaspoon garlic powder
1/4 teaspoon oregano
1/8 teaspoon red pepper
3 tablespoons tamari
2 garlic cloves, diced

In a large skillet, heat the oil over medium-high heat; add the onions, celery, peppers, and mushrooms, and saute for 3 to 4 minutes. Add the cabbage and saute for 5 minutes, until all the vegetables are tender.

Add the spinach, garlic and spices; stir well and cook for 4 minutes more. Serve immediately.

QUICK VEGETABLE SAUTE
Serves 4

5 cups vegetables (broccoli,
   string beans, cauliflower, etc.)
3 tablespoons oil
5 garlic cloves, diced
6 tablespoons tamari

1/2 teaspoon garlic powder
1/2 teaspoon oregano
1/2 teaspoon basil
1/2 teaspoon paprika

Combine the vegetables with 3 cups water in a large pot; place over medium heat and steam for approximately 7 minutes, till tender but firm. In a skillet, heat the oil over medium-high heat; add the diced garlic, tamari and seasonings, stirring constantly; cook till the garlic is brown, but do not burn.

Add the steamed vegetables and quick fry over high heat for 5 minutes, stirring constantly. Add a little more tamari and garlic powder. Cook for a minute, until the vegetables are tender.

BREADED EGGPLANT OR ZUCCHINI
Serves 6

2 or 3 eggplants, or 4 or 5 zucchini
1/2 cup oil
1-1/2 cups water
1/2 cup soy powder
4 tablespoons tamari
4 tablespoons tahini
1 tablespoon garlic powder
1 teaspoon basil
1 teaspoon oregano
1 cup whole wheat flour

1/2 cup bread crumbs
1/4 cup bran
1/4 cup wheat germ
1/4 cup sesame seeds
1/4 cup ground sunflower seeds
1 teaspoon sea salt
1 teaspoon garlic powder
1 teaspoon basil
1 teaspoon oregano

Preheat oven to 400 F. Peel and cut eggplant into 1/4-inch slices (zucchini doesn't need to be peeled). Oil a baking sheet well. Combine the water, soy powder, tamari, tahini, garlic powder, basil and oregano to make a liquid batter.

In a separate bowl, mix the remaining dry ingredients. Dip each eggplant slice into the liquid, then into the breading, and place on the baking sheet. Fill the sheet and bake for 3 or 4 minutes, until golden brown; turn over and bake for 3 or 4 minutes more. Repeat this process until all the eggplant slices are cooked.

Serve with a sauce, such as tomato and cheesy gravy.

BROILED CROOKNECK SQUASH – BREADED
Serves 3

5 yellow crookneck squash
1/2 to 3/4 cup bread crumbs, or a
　　mixture of wheat germ and bran
1/2 cup oil

1/4 cup tamari
1/4 teaspoon garlic powder
1/4 teaspoon paprika

Cut squash into 1/4-inch thick slices. Combine the oil, tamari, and spices, in a small bowl. Preheat oven to broil.

Dip each squash slice into the oil mixture; sprinkle bread crumbs on one side. Put on a baking sheet, bread-crumb-side up. Broil for 3 to 5 minutes, until soft, watching to prevent burning.

This recipe may be used with any summer type squash.

BREADED ONION RINGS
Serves 4

3 large onions
1/2 cup wheat germ
1/3 cup bran
1 cup whole wheat pastry flour
1/2 teaspoon oregano
1/2 teaspoon garlic powder

1/2 teaspoon sea salt
1/2 teaspoon basil
3 tablespoons tahini
6 tablespoons water
1 tablespoon tamari

Preheat oven to 350 F. Oil a cookie sheet well. Slice onions into 1/4-inch thick rings. In a medium size bowl, combine the wheat germ, bran, and flour; add the spices.

In a separate bowl, mix together the tahini, water, and tamari. Dip each onion ring into the liquid batter, then into breading, and place on the cookie sheet. When the sheet is full, bake for 7 minutes or until golden brown and crisp, testing with a fork to see that they are soft. Turn rings over and bake for 7 minutes more.

Repeat process until all the onions are cooked.

BREADED STRING BEANS
Serves 4

1/2 cup bread crumbs
1/2 cup whole wheat flour
1/4 teaspoon parsley
1/4 teaspoon paprika
1/4 teaspoon garlic powder
1/4 teaspoon basil
1/4 teaspoon oregano

3 cups string beans
2 tablespoons oil
1 cup quick soy milk, or
   1 cup thin tahini dressing
   (see recipes)
3 to 4 tablespoons tamari

In a small bowl, combine the bread crumbs, flour and spices. In a large saucepan, combine the string beans and 2 cups water; steam over medium heat for 8 minutes, until they are soft but firm.

In a skillet, heat the oil over medium-high heat. Pour the soymilk into a small bowl. Dip 4 or 5 string beans into the soymilk, then into the bread crumbs; add to the skillet and turn with a spatula, adding a few diced garlic pieces and a sprinkle of tamari while cooking.

Keep turning for approximately 4 minutes, until they are toasted. Remove from the skillet. Repeat this procedure until all the string beans are cooked.

VARIATION

Substitute carrot strips or eggplant strips (no need to steam eggplant) for the string beans.

QUICK ZUCCHINI – STRING BEAN ITALIANO
Serves 4

6 tablespoons oil
5 garlic cloves, diced
1 large onion, sliced thin
1/4 cup tamari
3 to 4 zucchini, sliced
   into thin rounds

2 cups green beans, steamed
3 tablespoons roasted
   sesame seeds
1/2 cup bread crumbs
1/2 teaspoon garlic powder

Heat 2 tablespoons of the oil in a skillet over high heat, until very hot; add approximately 1/8 teaspoon of the diced garlic and 1/3 of the onion; saute for 3 or 4 minutes.

Add a dash of tamari and 1/3 of the sliced zucchini, stirring vigorously, and cook for 3 minutes. Add another dash of tamari and 1/8 teaspoon diced garlic; toss in 1/3 of the string beans, 1/3 of the sesame seeds, and 1/3 of the bread crumbs, stirring constantly. Add the garlic powder and season to taste. Cook for 3 or 4 minutes; transfer mixture to a bowl.

Repeat the above procedure until all the vegetables are cooked.

VARIATION

Substitute cauliflower for the zucchini.

STUFFED ARTICHOKES
Serves 4

3 whole fresh artichokes
2 cups water
3 tablespoons oil
1/4 cup chives, chopped
1/2 cup bread crumbs
1/4 cup sesame seeds

1/4 cup wheat germ
3 teaspoons tamari
1/2 teaspoon garlic powder
1/4 teaspoon basil
1/4 teaspoon oregano
1/4 teaspoon sea salt

In a large pot, combine the artichokes and 2 cups water; steam over medium heat for 45 minutes, or until leaves pull out easily.

Preheat oven to 350 F. Combine the remaining ingredients in a medium sized bowl, to make the stuffing. Put a little of the mixture down in between each leaf until most of the outer part of the artichoke is stuffed. Place in a large baking dish and bake for 10 to 15 minutes. Serve with an Italian olive oil dressing (see recipe), to dip each petal into before eating.

STUFFED TOMATO WITH SOYBEANS
Serves 7

7 large tomatoes
2 tablespoons oil
3 garlic cloves, diced
1 carrot, diced
1 celery stalk, diced
2 green peppers, diced
4 tablespoons tamari
1/2 teaspoon garlic powder

2 tablespoons tahini or
  peanut butter
1/2 teaspoon basil
1/2 teaspoon oregano
1/2 teaspoon paprika
1/4 teaspoon sea salt
3 cups cooked soybeans

Preheat oven to 350 F. Cut tops off tomatoes, gently scoop out and save insides, leaving a 1/4-inch thick shell. Heat the oil in a skillet over medium-high heat; add the garlic, vegetables, and seasonings, and saute for 5 minutes till tender.

Mash the soy beans in a large bowl. Add the vegetables, tahini and tomato insides. Season to taste. Stuff the tomato shells with the mixture; bake for 10 minutes.

Serve topped with a cheesy yeast gravy (see recipe), sesame meal, or nutritional yeast, if desired.

VARIATION

Instead of baking, chill the mixture and serve in uncooked tomato shells.

FRIED BEANS
Serves 6

3 cups cooked pinto
   and/or kidney beans
2 tablespoons oil
3 garlic cloves, diced
3 large onions, chopped
2 tablespoons tamari

1/4 teaspoon sea salt
1/4 teaspoon oregano
Dash of crushed cumin seed
   or cumin powder
Dash of red pepper

In a skillet, heat the oil over medium-high heat; add the diced garlic and the onion, and saute for 5 minutes, until tender. Drain the beans and mash well; add to the saute. Reduce heat to low. Add the seasoning: the more Mexican style desired, the more cumin needed. Cook for 5 minutes more.

These beans are delicious served on tacos or corn bread with guacamole, lettuce, and tomato; or with brown rice.

BARBECUED BEANS
Serves 8

3 cups uncooked beans (pinto,
   lentils, navy, soy, etc.)
7 cups tomato stock or soup
1/4 cup tamari
1/8 cup oil
1 teaspoon garlic powder

1 teaspoon oregano
1 teaspoon basil
Dash of red pepper
2 onions, cut into chunks
1 whole bulb garlic, diced

Soak the beans overnight in sufficient water to cover.

In a large soup pot, combine the tomato stock, tamari, and oil; place over medium heat and bring to a boil. Add the beans; reduce heat and simmer for 3 to 4 hours, gradually adding the seasonings while cooking, the larger amounts toward the end of the cooking time. Add one of the onions and 4 cloves of diced garlic after one hour. If necessary, add more stock. Add the remaining cloves of diced garlic, the remaining onion, and a dash of pepper. The beans are ready when soft.

VARIATION

Baked beans—After cooking, drain beans (save liquid for stock or sauce base), and place in a casserole; add freshly diced garlic and onion. Bake at 350 F. For 45 minutes to an hour.

"Now what is it moves our very heart, and sickens us so much at cruelty shown to poor brutes? I suppose this: first, that they have done us no harm; next, that they have no power whatever to resistance; it is the cowardice and tyranny of which they are the victims which make their sufferings so especially touching; ...there is something so very dreadful, so Satanic in tormenting those who have never harmed us, and who cannot defend themselves, who are utterly in our power."

Cardinal Newman

(Upon being told by doctors that he would die if he refused to eat meat)

"My situation is a solemn one: Life is offered to me on the condition of eating beefsteaks. But death is better than cannibalism. My will contains directions for my funeral, which will be followed not by mourning coaches, but by oxen, sheep, flocks of poultry, and a small traveling aquarium of live fish, all wearing white scarves in honor of the man who perished rather than eat his fellow-creatures. It will be, with the exception of Noah's Ark, the most remarkable thing of its kind ever seen."

George Bernard Shaw

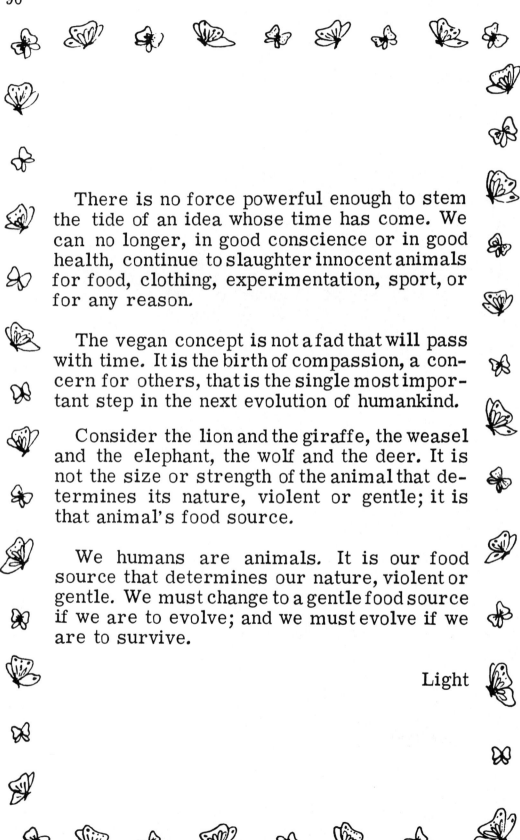

There is no force powerful enough to stem the tide of an idea whose time has come. We can no longer, in good conscience or in good health, continue to slaughter innocent animals for food, clothing, experimentation, sport, or for any reason.

The vegan concept is not a fad that will pass with time. It is the birth of compassion, a concern for others, that is the single most important step in the next evolution of humankind.

Consider the lion and the giraffe, the weasel and the elephant, the wolf and the deer. It is not the size or strength of the animal that determines its nature, violent or gentle; it is that animal's food source.

We humans are animals. It is our food source that determines our nature, violent or gentle. We must change to a gentle food source if we are to evolve; and we must evolve if we are to survive.

Light

"He will be regarded as a benefactor of his race who shall teach man to confine himself to a more innocent diet. Whatever my own practice may be, I have no doubt that it is a part of the destiny of the human race, in its gradual improvement, to leave off eating animals as surely as the savage tribes have left off eating each other. The faintest assured objection which one healthy man feels will at length prevail over the arguments and customs of mankind."

"No humane being past the thoughtless age of boyhood will wantonly murder any creature which holds its life the same tenure that he does."

Henry David Thoreau

"Animals are in our power in a peculiar sense;
they are committed by God to our sovereignty,
and we owe to them a considerate regard for their
rights. No animal life can be treated as a THING.
Willful disrespect of the sanctities of physical
life in one sphere, bears its fruits in other and
higher spheres."

Bishop Westcott

Main Dishes

Sautés
Grains
Casseroles
Burgers

BEET SAUTE
Serves 4

2 tablespoons oil
2 onions, sliced
1 bunch of beets with tops, sliced
2 stalks celery, diced
4 garlic cloves, diced

2 tablespoons tamari
1/2 teaspoon sea salt
1/2 teaspoon garlic powder
1/4 teaspoon basil

In a large skillet heat the oil over medium heat; add the onions, stirring well. Add the beets, celery, garlic and beet tops, mixing well after each addition. Add the seasonings. Continue to saute, stirring constantly, for 5 minutes or until the vegetables are tender.

VARIATION

The beets can be grated before sauteing.

CABBAGE AND NOODLES
Serves 4

2 tablespoons oil
2 garlic cloves, diced
2 large onions, sliced
2 stalks celery, diced
2 peppers, sliced
1 head of cabbage, sliced thin

1/4 cup tamari
1/2 teaspoon garlic powder
1/2 teaspoon sea salt
2 cups cooked noodles
5 or 6 tablespoons tomato sauce
  (see recipe)

Heat the oil in a large skillet over high heat. Add the onions and garlic, and saute for 3 minutes, until onions are transparent.

Add the celery and peppers; saute for 3 or 4 minutes. Add the seasonings; reduce heat. Add the cabbage; saute for 4 minutes more. Stir in the noodles and sauce. Simmer for 5 minutes and serve.

CURRIED CAULIFLOWER
Serves 4 to 6

1 large head cauliflower
2 cups water
3 tablespoons oil
3 to 5 garlic cloves, diced

4 tablespoons tamari
2 to 3 large onions, thinly sliced
1/2 teaspoon curry powder

Cut the cauliflower into bite-size pieces; place in a saucepan with the water. Steam the cauliflower for 5 to 7 minutes over medium heat, till slightly soft.

In a wok or skillet, heat the oil over high heat; add 3 or 4 of the cloves of garlic, the tamari and the onions, and saute for 3 or 4 minutes, stirring constantly. Add the cauliflower; saute for 2 or 3 minutes. Add the curry powder and 1 or 2 more garlic cloves and a dash of tamari; saute for 5 minutes more.

CAULIFLOWER MUSHROOM
Serves 4

2 tablespoons oil
2 large onions, cut into quarters
1 head cauliflower,
   cut into bite size pieces

1 cup fresh mushrooms, sliced
3 tablespoons tamari
1/2 teaspoon garlic powder

Heat the oil in a skillet over high heat; add the onions, and saute for 3 minutes until golden. Add the cauliflower; saute for 8 minutes.

Add the mushrooms and continue cooking for 3 minutes until the vegetables are golden brown. Add the tamari. Let simmer 3 minutes. Season to taste.

PEPPERS AND ONIONS
Serves 6

3 tablespoons oil
4 garlic cloves, diced
5 to 6 onions, sliced
8 green peppers, sliced

5 to 6 tablespoons tamari
1/4 teaspoon basil
Dash of ginger powder
Dash of sea salt

Heat the oil in a large skillet over medium-high heat; add the garlic and onions, and saute for 3 minutes until light brown.

Add the remaining ingredients; saute for 3 minutes more until the peppers are soft. Serve with rice, millet, or chunks of potato.

This delicious dish is easy to prepare.

BROCCOLI-CABBAGE SAUTE
Serves 6

2 tablespoons oil
2 large onions, sliced
3 garlic cloves, minced
2 celery stalks, diced
1 carrot, sliced
2 peppers, sliced
1 bunch broccoli, cut into chunks

1/2 head cabbage,
   sliced into thin strips
5 tablespoons tamari
1/4 teaspoon garlic powder
1/4 teaspoon sea salt
1/4 teaspoon basil
1/8 teaspoon oregano

In a large skillet, heat the oil over medium heat; add the onions and garlic, and saute for 3 minutes, until golden. Add the celery, carrots, and peppers; saute for 2 to 4 minutes.

Add the broccoli and cabbage, and the seasonings to taste. Saute for 10 minutes; don't overcook, vegetables should be tender yet firm. The total cooking time is approximately 20 minutes.

VARIATION

5 minutes before saute is done, dilute 3 tablespoons tahini in saute stock and add to vegetables.

EGGPLANT TAHINI SAUTE
Serves 4 to 6

2 tablespoons oil
3 large onions, sliced
2 carrots, sliced
4 stalks celery, chopped
2 eggplants, peeled
  and cut into chunks
4 tablespoons tamari

3/4 cup thick tahini dressing
  (see recipe)
3 garlic cloves, diced
1/2 teaspoon basil
1/4 teaspoon sea salt
1/4 teaspoon garlic powder
1/8 teaspoon red pepper

In a large skillet, heat the oil over medium-high heat; add all the vegetables (adding the eggplant last, after the celery starts to get tender), and saute for 7 minutes. Add the seasonings, and continue cooking for 4 minutes more, till the eggplant is tender. Add the tahini dressing.

Season to taste; stir, reduce heat and cover; simmer for 4 to 5 minutes.

VARIATION

Substitute zucchini or cabbage for the eggplant.

EGGPLANT GOULASH
Serves 4 to 6

3 tablespoons oil
2 garlic cloves, diced
2 onions, sliced
3 celery stalks, chopped
3 carrots, sliced into rounds
2 potatoes, cut into chunks
1 cup cauliflower (optional),
  broken into flowerettes
1/2 teaspoon sea salt

1/2 teaspoon garlic powder
1/2 teaspoon oregano
1/2 teaspoon basil
2 green peppers, chopped
2 eggplants, peeled and cut into
  bite size pieces
1/2 cup green peas, or
  1/2 cup green beans, sliced
1 cup tomato sauce (see recipe)

Heat the oil in a large skillet over medium heat; add the garlic and onions, and saute for 4 or 5 minutes. Add the celery, carrots, potatoes, and cauliflower. Add half the spices; cover and cook for 10 minutes.

Add the peppers, eggplants, and peas or beans. Add the remaining spices and the tomato sauce; simmer for 3 or 4 minutes.

Serve alone or over rice or noodles.

LENTIL LEEK SAUTE
Serves 4 to 6

4 cups stock or water
2 cups lentils
2 tablespoons oil
1 bunch leeks
3 garlic cloves, diced
3 tablespoons tamari

1/2 teaspoon sea salt
1/4 teaspoon garlic powder
1/4 teaspoon basil
1/4 teaspoon oregano
2 tablespoon sesame seeds

Put the water and lentils in a large saucepan; place over medium heat and cook for approximately 30 minutes, until soft.

Heat the oil in a large skillet over medium heat; add the leeks, garlic, and seasonings to taste. Saute for 3 minutes, till leeks are tender; add the lentils and sesame seeds. Cook for 5 minutes more and season to taste.

MUSHROOM MUNG BEAN SAUTE
Serves 4

2 tablespoons of oil
2 onions, sliced into rings
3 cloves garlic, diced
2 tablespoons tamari
1/2 pound mushrooms

1 cup mung bean sprouts
1/4 cup stock
1/4 teaspoon sea salt
1/4 teaspoon garlic powder

Heat the oil in a large skillet; add the onions, garlic and tamari. Saute for 5 minutes until tender. Add the mushrooms, stock, and seasonings; cook for 3 minutes more, and add bean sprouts, mixing well. Cover and allow to sit for 5 minutes before serving.

VARIATION

Add 1 8-ounce cake of tofu, diced, with the mushrooms.

ONION, CABBAGE, CARROT QUICKIE
Serves 4 to 6

2 tablespoons oil
3 garlic cloves, diced
3 onions, sliced
3 carrots, sliced thin
1 stalk celery, diced
1 pepper, sliced

1 head cabbage, sliced thin
5 tablespoons tamari
1/2 teaspoon garlic powder
1/4 teaspoon sea salt
1/4 teaspoon basil
1/4 teaspoon oregano

Heat the oil in a large skillet over medium-high heat; add the garlic, onions, carrots, celery, and pepper. Saute for 5 minutes, till almost tender. Add the cabbage; saute for 5 minutes more; stir often, and add more oil if necessary.

Add the seasonings to taste. Cook for 5 minutes more, till vegetables are tender but firm— approximately 15 minutes total.

POTATO-CABBAGE COMBO
Serves 4

2 tablespoons oil
2 large onions, sliced
4 medium potatoes, cut into chunks
1/2 head cabbage, sliced
2 garlic cloves, diced

3 tablespoons tamari
1/2 teaspoon sea salt
1/2 teaspoon basil
1/2 teaspoon oregano

Heat the oil in a large skillet over medium-high heat; add onions and potatoes, and saute for 7 minutes.

Add the cabbage, garlic, tamari, and spices. Cook for 5 minutes more, till potatoes and cabbage are tender.

ITALIAN SAUTE
Serves 4 to 6

1/2 head broccoli,
   cut into chunks
1/2 head cauliflower,
   cut into chunks
2 cups string beans, sliced
1 pound asparagus
3 tablespoons oil

5 garlic cloves, diced
4 tablespoons tamari
1/4 teaspoon garlic powder
1/4 teaspoon oregano
1/4 teaspoon basil
1/4 teaspoon paprika
1/4 teaspoon sea salt

Steam the vegetables by placing them in a medium sized saucepan with 2 cups of water. Place over medium heat, and cook for about 7 minutes, till slightly tender.

Heat the oil in a large frying pan over medium heat; add the garlic and tamari, and cook until garlic is golden, stirring constantly. Add the steamed vegetables and the seasonings; cook over high heat for 3 minutes, stirring constantly; add a dash of tamari and garlic powder, while cooking until vegetables are tender but not soft.

TOFU SAUTE
Serves 4

2 tablespoons oil
3 garlic cloves, diced
3 large onions, sliced
2 stalks celery, cut into chunks
1 pepper, sliced
1/4 head cabbage, sliced
1 cup mung bean sprouts

2 8-ounce cakes tofu,
   cut into bite-size cubes
2 tablespoons tamari
1/2 teaspoon garlic powder
1/4 teaspoon oregano
1/4 teaspoon basil

Heat the oil in a large skillet over medium-high heat. Add the garlic, onions, celery, peppers, and cabbage; saute for 7 minutes, until almost soft.

Add the mung bean sprouts, tofu, and seasonings. Cook for 5 to 10 minutes, stirring often.

POTATOES WITH TOFU
Serves 5

2 tablespoons oil
3 onions, sliced
3 garlic cloves, diced
7 potatoes, baked or steamed,
　and sliced
1 8-ounce cake tofu, diced
1/2 pound of mushrooms, sliced

2 tablespoons nutritional yeast
3 tablespoons tamari
1/2 teaspoon garlic powder
1/2 teaspoon sea salt
1/2 teaspoon basil
1/2 teaspoon oregano

Heat the oil in a large skillet over medium-high heat; add the onions and garlic, and saute for 5 minutes.

Add the potatoes, tofu, mushrooms, yeast, and seasonings. Saute for 5 to 7 minutes more.

NOODLE TOFU
Serves 5

1 pound spaghetti (whole wheat,
　spinach, or Jerusalem artichoke)
2 quarts water
2 tablespoons oil
1 8-ounce cake tofu,
　cut into bite-size pieces

4 garlic cloves, minced
2 tablespoons tamari
1/4 teaspoon garlic powder
1/4 teaspoon basil
1/8 teaspoon ginger powder
2 tablespoons nutritional yeast

Cook the spaghetti in 2 quarts of boiling water for approximately 10 minutes, until medium tender. Drain, and rinse in cold water.

Heat the oil in a large skillet over medium heat; add the tofu, and saute for 3 minutes. Add 1/2 of the spaghetti, turning it with a spatula. Add 2 of the garlic cloves, stirring constantly; add 1 tablespoon of the tamari, and 1/2 of the seasonings. Sprinkle in 1 tablespoon of the nutritional yeast. Transfer this saute to a large casserole dish.

Repeat the entire operation with the remaining 1/2 of all the ingredients—this is done to prevent the mixture from becoming too mushy.

TOFU BEAN-THREAD SAUTE
Serves 4 or 5

1 4-ounce package bean threads
1 quart of boiling water
3 tablespoons oil
4 garlic cloves, diced
2 large onions, sliced
1 8-ounce cake tofu,
   cut into 1/4-inch strips
3 tablespoons tamari
1 celery stalk, cut into chunks

1 carrot, sliced thin
1 teaspoon fresh ginger, diced,
   or 1/4 teaspoon ginger powder
1 teaspoon garlic powder
1/2 teaspoon basil
1/4 teaspoon sea salt
2 peppers, cut into strips
2 tablespoons sesame seeds

Place the bean threads in 1 quart boiling water; when water reboils, the bean threads should be tender. Drain and rinse.

Heat the oil in a large skillet over medium-high heat; add the garlic and saute for 2 minutes, till golden. Add the onions and tofu, and saute for 3 minutes; add the tamari, stirring well.

Mix in the celery, carrots, and remaining spices; cook for 5 minutes. Add the peppers and bean threads; cook for 2 minutes, and season to taste.

Sprinkle with sesame seeds and serve.

BEAN THREADS AND GARLIC
Serves 4

1 4-ounce package of bean threads
1 quart of boiling water
2 tablespoons oil

3 garlic cloves, diced
3 tablespoons tamari
5 tablespoons nutritional yeast

Place the bean threads in one quart of boiling water; when water reboils, threads should be tender. Drain and rinse.

Heat the oil in a large skillet over medium heat; add the garlic, stirring well.

Add the bean threads and cook for 3 minutes, stirring constantly. Add the tamari, and season to taste, stirring with a spatula.

Sprinkle nutritional yeast on top and serve (with a tahini tamari sauce, if desired).

CHINESE MEDLEY
Serves 6 to 8

4 tablespoons oil
5 garlic cloves, diced
5 large onions, cut into chunks
4 stalks celery, cut into chunks
3 peppers, sliced
1/2 head cabbage, shredded
1/3 cup tamari

1/4 teaspoon ginger powder
1/8 teaspoon red pepper
1/4 teaspoon sea salt
1/2 teaspoon garlic powder
3 tablespoons arrowroot powder
1 cup mung bean sprouts

Heat the oil in a wok or skillet over high heat, until very hot; add 2 cloves of the garlic and all the onions. Saute for 5 minutes, stirring often.

Add the celery, peppers, and half of the spices; cook for 3 or 4 minutes. Add the cabbage and the remaining spices except for the garlic. Sift the arrowroot through a strainer or sifter, and sprinkle into the vegetables, stirring constantly.

Cook for 5 minutes, till the mixture thickens; then add the remaining garlic and the sprouts. Reduce heat, cover and simmer for 3 or 4 minutes before serving.

SWEET AND SOUR CABBAGE
Serves 8

2 tablespoons oil
1 garlic clove, diced
2 large onions, sliced
2 tablespoons tamari
2 heads cabbage, sliced very thin

1 large apple, shredded
1 tablespoon apple cider vinegar
4 tablespoons sorghum
Dash of garlic powder

Heat the oil in a large saucepan over medium heat, add the garlic and onions, and saute for 2 minutes. Add the tamari, cabbage, and apple, and cook for 7 minutes, stirring often.

Add the sorghum, vinegar, and garlic powder; reduce heat and simmer for half an hour.

Also delicious when stored for the following day. Great with mashed potatoes.

TEMPURA
Serves 4

1 quart peanut or sesame oil
  (has a low boiling point)

Batter

1/2 cup whole wheat flour
  (or 1/4 cup whole wheat and
  1/4 cup buckwheat flour)

1 teaspoon baking soda
2 to 3 tablespoons water

Vegetables

1 bunch broccoli,
  separated into flowerettes
1 eggplant, peeled and cut
  into slices 1/4-inch thick

2 onions, sliced into rings
1 cauliflower, cut into flowerettes
3 carrots, sliced into thin strips

In a medium size bowl, combine all the batter ingredients, adding just enough water to form a loose consistency.

Heat the oil to 450 F. in a large pot over medium-high heat. Dip each vegetable piece into the batter, and drop into the oil. Cook for approximately 3 minutes, until golden. The cooking time will vary with type of vegetable. Place in a colander to drain oil off.

Serve immediately with tamari as a dipping sauce.

BROWN RICE
Serves 4

3-1/2 cups water
2 cups brown rice,
   washed in cold water

1/4 cup tamari
1/4 cup oil

In a medium sized saucepan, bring the water to a boil; add the oil and tamari. Place the rice in the water and cover. When water boils again, reduce heat. Cook for 50 minutes, till all the water has been absorbed or evaporated. Remove from burner and allow to cool.

COUS COUS
Serves 3 or 4

1 cup cous cous

2 cups water

In a medium sized saucepan, bring the water to a boil; add the cous cous and reduce heat. Cook for approximately 20 minutes, until all water has been absorbed or evaporated.

If desired, season this with a sauce or dressing, such as cheesy gravy. Delicious as a side dish.

To make a breakfast cereal, just add 1/2 to 1 cup more water, for a looser consistency.

VARIATION

Cous cous with onions: Make a saute of onions, diced garlic, and tamari, and add to the cooked grain.

MILLET LOAF
Serves 6 to 8

3 cups millet
6 cups water
2 tablespoons oil
3 onions, diced
2 peppers, diced
2 celery stalks, diced
4 garlic cloves, diced
1 teaspoon garlic powder

1/2 teaspoon oregano
1/2 teaspoon basil
1/2 teaspoon sea salt
2 tablespoons tahini
1/4 cup wheat germ
2 cups tomato sauce (see recipe)
3 tablespoons nutritional yeast

Preheat oven to 350 F. Bring the water to a boil in a large pot. Add the millet and cook over medium heat for 25 minutes, or until all water is absorbed.

Heat the oil in a skillet, over medium-high heat; add the onions, peppers, celery, and fresh garlic, and saute for 5 minutes. Add the seasonings, and cook for 2 minutes more, till vegetables are tender; mix into the millet. Add the tahini and wheat germ, and half of the tomato sauce; mix well. Season to taste.

Shape into a mounded loaf in an 8" x 12" baking dish; pour remaining tomato sauce over loaf and sprinkle yeast on top. Bake for half hour. Serve in slices with tomato sauce.

MILLET
Serves 8

3 cups millet
5 tablespoons oil
5-1/2 cups water
1/4 cup tamari
2 onions, diced
4 garlic cloves, diced

1/2 teaspoon garlic powder
1/4 teaspoon basil
1/4 teaspoon oregano
1/4 teaspoon paprika
1/4 teaspoon sea salt

Preheat oven to 300 F. In a bowl, combine the millet and 3 tablespoons of the oil, mixing well. Spread mixture on a baking sheet and toast in the oven for 30 to 40 minutes, until golden. The toasting is not necessary, but it adds a nuttier flavor to the grain.

Bring to a boil in a large saucepan: the water, the remaining 2 tablespoons of oil, and the tamari. Add the millet, and reduce to low heat. Cover and cook for 25 to 35 minutes, until medium soft, adding 1 of the onions and 2 of the garlic cloves after 15 minutes of cooking.

When ready, remove pan from heat and add the remaining onion and garlic and the seasonings.

VARIATION

Make into a casserole by adding 1 cup tahini dressing, 1 cup freshly chopped vegetables, and 1/2 cup tomato sauce. Combine with the cooked millet, and place in a baking dish; cover with a thin layer of tahini dressing. Bake at 325 F. for 20 minutes until brown on top.

KASHA (BUCKWHEAT GROATS)
Serves 5

2 cups kasha
4 cups water
2 tablespoons oil
5 large onions, diced
2 carrots, diced
2 stalks celery, diced
4 garlic cloves, diced

1/3 cup tamari
1/2 teaspoon parsley
1/2 teaspoon garlic powder
1/2 teaspoon basil
1/4 teaspoon sea salt
1/8 teaspoon red pepper (optional)
3 tablespoons tahini

In a large saucepan, bring the water to a boil; add kasha and cook over low heat for 15 to 20 minutes, until soft.

Heat the oil in a skillet over medium-high heat; add the diced vegetables and garlic, and saute for 7 minutes until soft. Mix the kasha and add to the vegetables. Add the seasonings; add more oil if necessary. Add the tahini, and cook for 5 to 8 minutes.

FRIED RICE
Serves 6

4 cups cooked rice
1/3 cup oil
1/2 cup garlic cloves, diced

1/4 cup tamari
1/2 teaspoon ginger powder

Heat 2 tablespoons of the oil in a large skillet, over high heat. Add enough of the rice to cover the bottom, and fry it for 6 minutes till golden brown, while gradually reducing heat to medium, and stirring every 2 minutes. Use a spatula to turn the rice.

Add 1 teaspoon of the diced garlic, 1 tablespoon of the tamari, 1/8 teaspoon ginger, and seasoning to taste. When ready, place the rice in an 8" x 12" baking dish.

Repeat the process until all the rice is fried, continuing to fry in quantities that just cover the bottom of the pan.

RICE MEDLEY
Serves 4

2 cups cooked brown rice
2 tablespoons oil
7 garlic cloves, diced
5 large onions, sliced
2 celery stalks, diced
1 green pepper, diced

1/3 cup tamari
1/2 teaspoon sea salt
1/2 teaspoon sweet basil
1/4 teaspoon ginger
1/8 teaspoon red pepper
1 cup bean sprouts

Heat the oil in a large skillet. Add 5 of the garlic cloves, the onions, celery, and pepper, and 1/2 of the seasonings; saute for 5 minutes. Add remaining garlic and the sprouts, mixing well, and saute for 2 minutes. Add the rice and the remaining seasonings; the tamari gives it a "Chinesey" taste.

RICE TAHINI
Serves 8

2 tablespoons oil
6 large onions, sliced
7 garlic cloves, diced
5 stalks celery, chopped
5 tablespoons tamari
1/2 teaspoon garlic powder
1/4 teaspoon basil

1/4 teaspoon oregano
1/4 teaspoon sea salt
1/4 teaspoon paprika
1/2 cup carrot, grated
2 green peppers, diced
3 cups cooked brown rice
2 cups tahini dressing (see recipe)

Preheat oven to 350 F. Heat the oil in a large skillet over medium-high heat; add the onions and garlic, and saute for 3 minutes, till tender. Add the celery, tamari, and spices; cook for 5 minutes. Add the carrot and green peppers, and cook for 2 minutes more. Remove pan from heat, and mix the rice in.

Oil an 8" x 12" baking dish; add 1/2 of the rice mixture and pour a layer of tahini dressing over it. Add the remaining rice on top and cover with tahini dressing. Bake for 30 to 45 minutes, until top is golden brown.

SPANISH RICE
Serves 2

2 cups water
1 cup brown rice
1 tablespoon olive oil
3 tablespoons tamari
1/2 teaspoon sea salt

1/2 teaspoon paprika
1/3 teaspoon saffron
1/2 cup green peas
2 tomatoes, cut into wedges
1 onion, diced

Preheat oven to 350 F. Bring the water to a boil in a medium sized saucepan. Add the rice, olive oil, tamari and seasonings. Cover, reduce heat and simmer for 45 minutes, until all the water is absorbed.

Transfer the rice to a casserole dish: garnish with peas, tomatoes and onion; or alternate layers of rice, peas, tomatoes and onion. Bake for 20 minutes.

STUFFED CABBAGE
Serves 6 to 8

2 tablespoons oil
4 garlic cloves, diced
4 large onions, diced
2 carrots, grated
2 stalks celery, diced
1 green pepper, diced
5 tablespoons tamari
1/2 teaspoon sea salt
1/2 teaspoon basil

1/2 teaspoon garlic powder
1/2 teaspoon oregano
2 large heads of cabbage
4 cups cooked grain (millet, rice, kasha, etc.)
6 tablespoons tahini or peanut butter
1/2 teaspoon paprika

Heat the oil in a large skillet over medium-high heat; add the garlic, onions, carrots, celery, pepper and all of the spices except the paprika. Saute for 5 minutes, until tender.

In a large pot or two medium sized pots, combine the whole cabbage heads with 2 cups of water; place over medium heat and steam for 8 minutes, until soft but firm.

Combine the grain and the sauteed vegetables, including their juice; season to taste. Add the tahini to finish the filling.

Preheat oven to 350 F.

Remove the cabbage leaves one at a time, lay each leaf out flat and fill with 2 to 3 heaping tablespoons of the filling. Roll the leaf up, pushing the ends inside the roll. Cover the bottom of an 8" x 12" baking dish with tomato sauce; place the rolled cabbage leaves in it, and top with more sauce. Sprinkle the paprika on top and bake for 30 minutes. Serve with extra tomato sauce on the side.

VARIATION

Top with cheesy gravy (see recipe).

STUFFED PEPPERS
Serves 10

2 tablespoons oil
4 garlic cloves, diced
2 large onions, diced
1 stalk celery, diced
2 carrots, diced
1 green pepper, diced
5 tablespoons tamari
1/2 teaspoon basil
1/2 teaspoon sea salt
Dash of pepper

1/2 teaspoon paprika
1/2 teaspoon oregano
3 cups cooked rice, or
   1-1/2 cups cooked millet and
   1-1/2 cups cooked rice
3 tablespoons tahini
   or peanut butter
6 to 10 green peppers,
   seeded and cored

Preheat oven to 350 F. Heat the oil in a large skillet over medium-high heat. Add the garlic, onions, celery, carrots, pepper, tamari, and the other spices; saute for 5 minutes until tender. Add to the grain (leftover baked grain may also be used as a filling). Add the tahini, and season to taste.

Stuff each pepper almost to the top with mix; place them on a baking sheet. Bake for 20 to 30 minutes until the peppers are soft.

VARIATION

Use the filling to stuff tomatoes and mushrooms in place of the peppers.

SIMPLE VEGETABLE BAKE
Serves 4 or 5

2 onions. cut into chunks
2 medium potatoes, cut into chunks
2 carrots, sliced
2 red peppers, sliced
2 garlic cloves, diced
1/4 teaspoon garlic powder

1/4 teaspoon oregano
1/4 teaspoon basil
1-1/2 cups tomato sauce,
  or oil tamari dressing,
  or tahini dressing
(see recipes)

Preheat oven to 375 F. In a large casserole dish, combine all the ingredients, except the sauce. Pour the sauce over the mixture. Cover and bake for 30 to 45 minutes, stirring occasionally to prevent burning.

VARIATION

Substitute other vegetables, such as: corn kernels, broccoli, **squash**, sweet potatoes, cauliflower, etc.

BARLEY CASSEROLE
Serves 6

2 cups barley
6 cups water
2 tablespoons oil
2 large onions, sliced
5 garlic cloves, diced
2 carrots, grated
2 stalks celery, diced

5 tablespoons tamari
1/4 teaspoon sea salt
1/4 teaspoon basil
1/4 teaspoon oregano
1/4 teaspoon garlic powder
3/4 cup tahini dressing
  (see recipe)

Preheat oven to 350 F. Bring the water to a boil in a large saucepan; add the barley and cook for approximately 45 minutes, until soft.

Heat the oil in a large skillet over medium-high heat; add the onions and garlic, and saute for 5 minutes until tender. Add the carrots and celery; season with the tamari, sea salt, basil, oregano, and garlic powder. Cook for 5 minutes, until the vegetables are tender. Add the barley and saute for 3 minutes. Season to taste.

Transfer half of the mixture to an 8'' x 12'' baking dish; add a layer of tahini dressing. Top with another layer of barley mixture and dressing. Bake for 35 minutes.

CARROT CASSEROLE
Serves 5

6 carrots, sliced
2 large onions, chopped
4 garlic cloves, diced
1 eggplant, peeled, cut into chunks
1 crookneck squash, diced
2 cups water
2 tablespoons oil
1 large pepper, chopped
1 stalk celery, cut into chunks

3 tablespoons tamari
1/2 teaspoon garlic powder
1/2 teaspoon basil
1/2 teaspoon sea salt
1/4 teaspoon dill weed
3 tablespoons peanut butter
1/2 cup tahini dressing (see recipe)
1/2 teaspoon paprika
(for top decoration)

In a large pot, combine the carrots, 1 of the onions, 2 cloves of the garlic, the eggplant, squash, and 2 cups of water. Place over medium heat and steam for 10 minutes, until soft. Drain and mash well. Add 1/2 the spices; add the peanut butter; mix well. Season to taste.

Heat the oil in a medium-sized frying pan. Put in it: the remaining onion, garlic, and seasonings; also the pepper and celery. Saute for 5 minutes until the vegetables are tender. Add the saute to the steamed vegetables, mixing well.

Preheat oven to 350 F. Oil 8" x 12" baking dish. Pour mixture into baking dish. Top with dressing and paprika. Bake for 35 minutes.

VARIATION

Instead of combining the mashed steamed vegetables and saute, place them in the baking dish in alternating layers, including the dressing as a layer.

CAULIFLOWER CASSEROLE
Serves 6

2 heads cauliflower
2 cups water
2 tablespoons oil
5 garlic cloves, diced
2 onions, cut into chunks
1/4 cup oil
1/4 cup tamari

3 teaspoons sesame seeds
1 teaspoon garlic powder
1/2 teaspoon basil
1/2 teaspoon oregano
1 8-ounce cake tofu,
    cut into chunks (optional)
1 onion, sliced (optional)

Preheat oven to 350 F. Break the cauliflower into large flowerettes. Add the water and steam over medium heat for 10 minutes until tender but firm.

Heat the oil in a small pan; add the garlic and onions, and saute for 5 minutes, till golden brown.

Combine the remaining ingredients, except the tofu, in a jar and mix well to make the dressing. Pour over the cauliflower and toss. Add the tofu and the saute, toss again. Transfer to 8" x 12" casserole dish. Top with sliced onion, if desired. Bake for 20 minutes.

CAULIFLOWER BROCCOLI CHEESE BAKE
Serves 6 to 8

1 head cauliflower,
   cut into flowerettes
1 bunch broccoli,
   cut into flowerettes
1 carrot, cut into thin rounds
2 tablespoons oil
3 garlic cloves, diced
2 onions, sliced

3 tablespoons tamari
1/2 teaspoon sea salt
1/2 teaspoon garlic powder
3 to 4 cups nutritional yeast gravy
   (see recipe)
1 tablespoon nutritional yeast
   powder
1 teaspoon paprika

Heat the oil in a large skillet, add the garlic, onions, cauliflower, broccoli and carrot; saute for 7 minutes. Add the tamari, sea salt, and garlic powder; cook for 3 minutes more.

Preheat oven to 400 F. In an 8" x 12" casserole dish, place alternating layers of gravy and saute mixture, finishing with layer of gravy. Sprinkle with nutritional yeast and paprika. Bake for 30 minutes.

CHICK-PEA LOAF
Serves 6 to 8

3 cups chick-peas
8 cups water
2 tablespoons oil
5 garlic cloves, diced
4 onions, diced
3 stalks celery, chopped
2 carrots, grated
1/4 cup tamari
2 tablespoons parsley, chopped

1 teaspoon cumin powder
1/2 teaspoon garlic powder
1/2 teaspoon sea salt
1/4 teaspoon turmeric
3 tablespoons tahini
   or peanut butter
1/4 cup tomato sauce
   (optional – see recipe)

Preheat oven to 375 F. Place the chick-peas in a large pot with water to cover and allow to soak for 3 to 4 hours or overnight before cooking. Drain water. Using medium heat, cook chick-peas in 8 cups of water, till soft (1-1/2 to 2 hours; or, approximately 1 hour in pressure cooker). Drain the liquid off, and mash the chick-peas well.

Heat the oil in a large skillet; add the garlic and onions, and saute for 5 minutes, till tender. Add the celery, carrot, tamari, and seasoning; saute for 5 minutes more, till vegetables are tender. Add to the mashed chick-peas and mix well. Add the remaining ingredients.

Oil two 8" x 8" baking dishes; divide the chick-pea mixture between the two pans. Sprinkle paprika on top. Bake for 30 minutes, or serve as is without baking. Also delicious cold.

MILLET BAKE
Serves 8

7-3/4 cups water
1/4 cup tamari
4 cups millet
2 tablespoons oil
5 garlic cloves, diced
5 large onions, diced
2 carrots, diced
2 green peppers, diced
1/2 teaspoon garlic powder
1/2 teaspoon sea salt
1/2 teaspoon basil

1/2 teaspoon parsley
1/4 teaspoon oregano
1/4 teaspoon paprika
1/8 teaspoon tarragon
1/2 cup tahini
2 tablespoons peanut butter
  (optional)
1/4 cup flour
1/2 cup tahini dressing
  (see recipe)

Put the water and tamari in a large pot, place over medium heat, and bring to a boil. Add the millet, reduce heat, and simmer for 25 to 30 minutes, until millet is fluffy and soft. Add more water if necessary.

Meanwhile, heat the oil in a large skillet over medium-high heat; add 3 garlic cloves and the onions; saute for 2 to 3 minutes. Add the carrots, celery and peppers; cook until all the vegetables are tender. Add remaining garlic and the seasonings.

Combine the millet and the sauteed vegetables in a large bowl. Add the tahini, peanut butter, and flour. Season to taste. If the mixture is too dry, add 1/4 cup vegetable stock or water.

Preheat oven to 350 F. Oil the bottom of an 8" x 12" baking dish, and add the millet mixture. Top with tahini dressing and bake for 35 minutes.

POTATOES AU GRATIN
Serves 7

2 tablespoons oil
2 large onions, sliced
1 celery stalk, sliced
1 carrot, diced (optional)
1/4 teaspoon garlic powder
1/4 teaspoon sea salt
4 tablespoons tamari

1-1/2 cups cheesy gravy
  (see recipe)
10 potatoes,
  baked, peeled and sliced,
  or steamed and sliced
1/2 teaspoon paprika
1 tablespoon nutritional yeast

Preheat oven to 350 F. Heat the oil in a large skillet over medium heat. Add the onions, celery, carrot and seasonings; cook for 7 minutes until vegetables are tender. Prepare the cheesy gravy.

In an 8" x 12" baking dish, alternate layers of gravy, potatoes, and sauteed vegetables; repeat. Top with gravy; sprinkle on paprika and nutritional yeast. Bake for 20 minutes.

POTATO KUGEL
Serves 6

10 potatoes, grated
1 large onion, diced
1/2 cup soy powder
3 tablespoons tamari
1/2 teaspoon garlic powder

1/2 teaspoon paprika
1/2 teaspoon basil
1/2 teaspoon sea salt
Dash of red pepper

Preheat oven to 350 F. Discard any potato water that has accumulated while grating.

In a large bowl, combine the potatoes, onion, soy powder, and spices. If too moist, add 1/3 cup bran, flour, or more soy powder. Oil an 8'' x 12'' casserole dish; put potato mixture in it. Bake for approximately 1 hour, checking it periodically. It should get golden brown on the top.

POTATO ZUCCHINI BAKE
Serves 6 to 8

2 tablespoons oil
2 garlic cloves, diced
2 onions, sliced
2 cups tahini/tamari sauce,
   or other type sauce
   (see recipes)

5 potatoes, baked,
   peeled and sliced;
   or steamed and sliced
2 zucchini, sliced 1/4'' thick
1 tablespoon nutritional yeast
1 teaspoon paprika

Heat the oil in a medium sized skillet, add the garlic and onions, and saute for 5 to 7 minutes. Preheat oven to 350 F.

In an 8'' x 12'' casserole, pour a thin layer of the sauce, place a layer of potatoes on top, then a layer of zucchini; cover with saute and another layer of sauce. Repeat the process. Sprinkle nutritional yeast and paprika on top. Bake for 20 to 30 minutes.

PUMPKIN CARROT CASSEROLE
Serves 6 to 8

1 small pumpkin,
  peeled and cut into chunks
1 pound carrots,
  peeled and sliced
3 tablespoon oil
3 garlic cloves, diced
3 large onions, diced
2 stalks celery, diced

1/3 cup tamari
1 teaspoon garlic powder
1/4 teaspoon oregano
1/4 teaspoon basil
1/4 teaspoon paprika
1 cup bran, wheat germ,
  or bread crumbs
1/2 cup peanut butter

In a large pot, combine the pumpkin and carrots with 3 cups water, and steam over medium heat for 20 minutes, until tender. Drain, conserving liquid for soup stock. Mash the pumpkin and carrots together until smooth.

In a frying pan, heat the oil over medium heat; add the diced garlic, onions, and celery; cook for 7 minutes until the vegetables are tender. Add the seasoning. Preheat oven to 350 F.

Add the sauteed vegetables to the pumpkin and carrot, and mix well. Mix in the bran and peanut butter. If the consistency is too loose, add 1/4 cup flour. Transfer mixture to an 8" x 12" baking dish; top with a thin coating of oil. Bake for 35 to 40 minutes.

STRING BEAN CHEESE BAKE
Serves 6

1 pound string beans,
  cut into bite sized pieces
2 tablespoons oil
2 onions, diced
2 carrots, diced
1 celery stalk, diced
3 garlic cloves, diced
4 tablespoons tamari

1 teaspoon sea salt
1/2 teaspoon garlic powder
2 to 3 cups vegetable stock or water
2/3 cup nutritional yeast
2 tablespoons nut butter
1/4 cup flour
1/2 teaspoon paprika

Place the string beans in a saucepan with 2 cups of water; cook over medium heat for 15 minutes, then drain and reserve the liquid. Heat the oil in a skillet over medium heat; add the onions, carrots, celery, and 2 of the garlic cloves, and saute for 7 minutes. Add 2 tablespoons of the tamari, 1/2 teaspoon of sea salt, and 1/4 teaspoon of garlic powder.

In a blender, combine the liquid with the remaining garlic clove, 2 onion slices, nutritional yeast, nut butter, flour, and the remaining tamari, sea salt, and garlic powder. Blend at high speed for 1 minute, until dressing is creamy —it will solidify when baked.

Preheat oven to 350 F. In a large bowl, mix the string beans with the sauteed vegetables and the dressing. Transfer to an 8" x 12" casserole dish; sprinkle top with nutritional yeast. Bake for 15 minutes.

VARIATION

Add peas to the casserole prior to baking.

SQUASH BAKE
Serves 6

4 or 5 squash (butternut, acorn,
    or scallop), peeled and
    cut into chunks
4 potatoes, cut into chunks
2 tablespoons oil
4 carrots, diced
2 peppers, diced
4 stalks celery, diced
3 onions, diced
1/4 cup tamari

4 garlic cloves, diced
1/2 teaspoon basil
1/2 teaspoon oregano
1/2 teaspoon garlic powder
5 tablespoons peanut butter
1 cup bran
1/2 to 1 cup flour
1/4 cup tahini
1/4 cup sesame seeds

Place squash and potatoes in a pressure cooker with 2 cups water. Cook approximately 4 minutes after the pressure is up, until tender. If not pressure cooked, steam for about 20 to 30 minutes.

While that is cooking, heat the oil in a large skillet over medium heat; add vegetables and saute for 7 minutes. Add the seasonings. Preheat oven to 375 F.

When ready, drain the squash and potatoes, and mash well. Add the sauteed vegetables and remaining ingredients. The batter should be fairly thick and creamy. If mixture is too wet, add 1 cup more flour. Place in an 8'' x 12'' baking dish; bake for 30 minutes. Brush with oil on the top to help make a crust. Sprinkle with paprika.

If desired, this bake can be made into burgers.

PUMPKIN POTATO CASSEROLE
Serves 6 to 8

8 large potatoes, cut into chunks
1/2 medium sized pumpkin or
    winter squash, peeled and
    cut into chunks
1 cup tahini dressing (see recipe)
2 tablespoons oil
5 large onions, diced
4 garlic cloves, minced

3 celery stalks, diced
1/2 teaspoon basil
1/2 teaspoon garlic powder
1/2 teaspoon oregano
1/4 teaspoon sea salt
1/4 teaspoon paprika
    (for top decoration)

Put potatoes and pumpkin in a large pot with 3 cups water. Steam over medium heat for 30 minutes, until soft. Drain the liquid off; then mash. Add the tahini dressing, and mix well.

Heat the oil in a frying pan over medium heat; add the onions, garlic, and celery. Saute for 7 minutes until soft, adding the seasonings while sauteing. Combine the sauteed vegetables and the potato mixture. Season to taste. Preheat oven to 350 F.

Oil two 8'' x 8'' baking pans; divide the mixture between the two pans. Brush the top of each casserole with oil and sprinkle with paprika. Bake for 20 minutes. Broil for 3 to 4 minutes, watching closely, until tops are golden brown.

BROCCOLI TAHINI BAKE
Serves 6 to 8

3 to 4 bunches broccoli
2 tablespoons oil
5 large onions, sliced
3 garlic cloves, diced
2 cups tahini sauce (see recipe)

2 tablespoons tamari
1/2 teaspoon garlic powder
1/2 teaspoon paprika
 (for top decoration)

Break the broccoli stalks apart, and put them in a large pot with 2 cups water. Place over medium heat and steam for 15 minutes until tender but not mushy.

Meanwhile, heat the oil in a skillet over medium heat; add the onions and garlic, and saute for 5 minutes, adding the tamari and seasoning to taste while cooking. Preheat oven to 350 F.

In an 8" x 12" baking dish, place a thin layer of broccoli; top this with a layer of onions, then tahini sauce; repeat to use all the ingredients. Sprinkle paprika on top and bake for 30 minutes.

VARIATION

Substitute asparagus, cauliflower, or anything your imagination will allow, for the broccoli.

CABBAGE-CARROT TAHINI BAKE
Serves 6 to 8

2 tablespoons oil
2 to 3 onions, sliced
3 garlic cloves, diced
1-1/2 pounds carrots,
 sliced to thin rounds
3 tablespoons tamari

1 teaspoon garlic powder
1 teaspoon basil
1 head cabbage, shredded
1-1/2 cups thick tahini dressing
 (see recipe)
1 teaspoon paprika

Heat the oil in a skillet over medium heat; add the onions, garlic and carrots, and saute for 3 to 4 minutes. Add the seasonings and the cabbage; cook for 5 minutes, until tender.

Place half of this saute into an 8" x 12" baking dish; cover with tahini dressing. Add the remaining saute and another layer of dressing. Sprinkle paprika on top.

VARIATION

Substitute different vegetables for the carrots. Use any type of thick sauce for the topping; (such as tomato, or cheesy gravy).

EGGPLANT TAHINI BAKE
Serves 6 to 8

2 tablespoons oil
6 large onions, sliced
1/4 cup tamari
1/2 teaspoon garlic powder
1/4 teaspoon paprika
1/4 teaspoon parsley

1/4 teaspoon basil
1/4 teaspoon oregano
3 garlic cloves, diced
1 cup tahini
2-1/2 cups water
4 eggplants, peeled and sliced thin

Heat the oil in a large frying pan over medium-high heat. Add the onions, 2 tablespoons of the tamari, the seasonings, and the diced garlic.

In a medium sized bowl, combine the tahini, remaining tamari, and water; mix well, until creamy and not watery. Add seasonings, if desired. Preheat oven to 350 F.

In two 8" x 12" baking dishes, pour a thin layer of tahini sauce, to prevent sticking; add a layer of eggplant, and a thin layer of sauteed onions. Cover with tahini sauce, and repeat layering. Sprinkle paprika on top of last layer of sauce. Bake for 45 minutes, until eggplant is tender (test with a fork).

Delicious served cold in a sandwich.

ONION TAHINI BAKE
Serves 4

5 large onions
1 cup bran
2 cups tahini dressing (see recipe)

2 tablespoons tamari
1/2 teaspoon oregano
1/2 teaspoon garlic powder

Preheat oven to 375 F. Slice the onions into long, thin slices. In a medium-size bowl, combine the dressing and bran; add the onions. Season with tamari, oregano, and garlic powder. Transfer mixture to an 8" x 8" baking dish, and bake for 20 minutes.

VARIATION

Saute onions before baking. Add pieces of soft tomato and slices of zucchini, if desired.

EGGPLANT PARMESAN
Yields 2 or 3 bakes

4 quarts tomato sauce (see recipe)
6 large eggplants, peeled,
    sliced thin and breaded
    (see breaded eggplant recipe)

1 cup tahini dressing, thick
    (see recipe)
4 cups cheese topping
    (see recipe)

Preheat oven to 350 F. Using 8" x 12" baking dishes, place a thin layer of tomato sauce on the bottom; add a layer of breaded eggplant, tomato sauce, and dab on a layer of cheese topping. Repeat: eggplant, sauce, and cheese. Top with 1/2 cup of tahini dressing. Bake for 35 to 40 minutes.

Serve with a side dish of tomato sauce.

EGGPLANT MILANESE
Serves 4 to 6

1 quart tomato sauce (see recipe)
2 large eggplants, peeled and sliced
1 large onion, cut into rings

2 green peppers, sliced
3 large garlic cloves, diced

Preheat oven to 350 F. In an 8" x 12" baking pan, pour a thin layer of tomato sauce. Using 1 eggplant, add a layer of eggplant slices, one layer of all the onion rings, and one layer of all the green peppers. Sprinkle diced garlic on top. Cover with tomato sauce, another layer of eggplant, and more sauce. Bake in the oven for approximately 1 hour, until vegetables are soft, testing with a fork.

Serve with yeast sauce on top (see recipe), if desired.

VARIATION

Add 1/2 cup tahini to tomato sauce for a cheesy flavor.

EGGPLANT YEAST BAKE
Serves 6

2 tablespoons oil
2 garlic cloves, diced
3 large onions, sliced
4 tablespoons tamari
1/2 teaspoon garlic powder
1/2 teaspoon basil
1/2 teaspoon sea salt

3 tablespoons whole wheat flour
1/2 to 3/4 cup nutritional yeast
1 cup vegetable stock or water
3 tablespoons tahini
1 large eggplant, peeled and
    cut into 1/4-inch thick rounds
1/4 teaspoon paprika

Heat the oil in a frying pan over medium heat; add the garlic and onions, and saute for 5 minutes. Season with 1 tablespoon of the tamari, 1/4 teaspoon of garlic powder, 1/4 teaspoon basil, and 1/4 teaspoon sea salt.

In a small saucepan, combine the flour and nutritional yeast. Add the stock, tahini, remaining tamari, garlic powder, basil, and sea salt; mix well. Place over low heat, and cook slowly for 15 minutes, stirring frequently, until it thickens. If too thick, add more liquid. Preheat oven to 350 F.

Oil an 8" x 12" baking dish; pour in a layer of sauce, then a layer of sliced eggplant, a layer of sauteed onions, and a layer of the nutritional yeast. Repeat the layering. Sprinkle top with paprika. Bake for 30 minutes, until eggplant is soft (test with a fork).

MATZOH TOFU BAKE
Serves 4 to 6

4 sheets whole wheat matzoh
1 cup soymilk
2 8-ounce cakes tofu, sliced thin
Sprinkle of cinnamon

1/2 cup raisins, soaked in water
　　for 15 to 20 minutes and drained
1/4 cup liquid sweetener

Preheat oven to 350 F. Soak matzoh in the soymilk for 3 to 4 minutes to soften.

In an 8" square baking dish, pour in just enough of the soymilk to cover the bottom. Place 1 sheet of matzoh in the pan; add a layer of tofu slices, sprinkle with cinnamon, and top with a sprinkle of raisins. Repeat the layers until all the matzoh is used. Top with a sprinkle of cinnamon; pour the liquid sweetener over the dish. Bake for 30 minutes.

VEGETABLE LOAF
Serves 4

3 tablespoons oil
2 garlic cloves, diced
2 large onions, diced
2 green peppers, diced
2 stalks celery, diced
2 carrots, diced
1/2 pound fresh mushrooms,
　　chopped

2/3 cup tamari
1 teaspoon garlic powder
1 teaspoon sea salt
1/2 teaspoon parsley
1/8 teaspoon red pepper
4 large potatoes, cut into chunks
1/4 cup cashew milk

Dough

1/3 cup oil
3 tablespoons cold orange juice

1/2 teaspoon sea salt
1-1/2 cups whole wheat flour

In a skillet, heat the oil over medium heat; add the diced garlic, onions, green peppers, celery, carrots and mushrooms, and saute for 5 minutes. Season with half the seasonings.

In a large saucepan, combine the potatoes and 4 cups of water, and boil for 10 to 15 minutes, until tender. Drain and mash the potatoes. Add the cashew milk and whip with a wooden spoon. Add the saute and remaining seasonings. Mix well.

Place mixture in refrigerator to cool. Preheat oven to 375 F.

In a bowl, combine the oil, orange juice and salt. Gradually add the flour until mixture is the texture of pie dough, moist yet pliable. Roll the dough out on a floured board into a 6" x 8" rectangle. Spoon the cooled mixture into the center, allowing dough on all sides to fold over, completely covering the mixture.

Oil a cookie sheet; slide the folded dough onto it. Bake for 40 minutes, until golden brown. If desired, make 2 smaller loaves.

May be made and served as a side dish. Serve topped with mushroom sauce (see recipe).

VARIATION

Add broccoli, spinach, cauliflower to the sauteed vegetables.

GREENS AND POTATOES CASSEROLE
Serves 6

2 tablespoons oil
2 large onions, diced
1 celery stalk, diced
1 carrot, diced
2 garlic cloves, diced
3 tablespoons tamari
1/2 teaspoon sea salt
1/2 teaspoon garlic powder

7 potatoes
1 pound greens
  (spinach or Swiss chard)
2-1/2 cups water
1 cup tahini dressing (optional)
  (see recipe)
Sprinkle of nutritional yeast
  (optional)

Heat the oil in a large skillet over medium heat. Add the onions, celery, carrots, and garlic; season with the tamari, sea salt, and garlic powder. Cook for 7 minutes, stirring occasionally, until vegetables are tender.

While cooking, place the potatoes and greens in separate saucepans with 2 cups of water in the potatoes, and 1/2 cup of water in the greens. Steam the potatoes for 20 minutes, until soft; and the greens for 5 minutes. Mash the potatoes and mix into the saute. Preheat oven to 350 F.

In a large baking dish, alternate layers of the potato mixture and the greens. Top it with the tahini dressing and a sprinkle of yeast, if desired. Bake for 20 minutes.

STUFFED BAKED POTATOES
Serves 6

7 large potatoes
1/4 pound mushrooms, diced
1 onion, diced
1/4 cup tahini
1/4 cup oil
1/8 cup vegetable stock or water
4 tablespoons nutritional yeast

4 tablespoons tamari
1/2 teaspoon sea salt
1/4 teaspoon basil
1/4 teaspoon oregano
1/4 teaspoon paprika
2 tablespoons sesame seeds

Preheat oven to 400 F. Bake the potatoes for 45 minutes, or until soft. When done, cool and cut in half lengthwise. Reduce oven to 350 F.

Spoon the potatoes out of their shells into a medium sized bowl, gently, so as not to damage the skins. Mash the potatoes well. Mix in the mushrooms, onions, tahini, oil, stock, yeast, and seasonings. Transfer the potato mixture back into the skin shells. Brush top with oil; sprinkle with garlic powder, nutritional yeast, paprika, and sesame seeds. Bake for 15 minutes, or until golden on top.

CABBAGE BAKE
Serves 4 to 6

1 head of cabbage, sliced thin

3 cups carrot sauce (see recipe)

In a medium sized pot, steam the cabbage in 3 cups water for 15 minutes. Drain liquid. Preheat oven to 350 F.

Place cabbage in an 8" x 8" baking dish; mix in carrot sauce. Bake for 10 minutes.

BULGHUR BURGERS
Yields 1-1/2 to 2 dozen

4 cups water
2 cups bulghur
2 tablespoons oil
1 onion, diced
2 beets, grated

2 carrots, diced
1/2 head cabbage, chopped fine
3 tablespoons tamari
1 teaspoon garlic powder

In a large pot, heat the water to a boil. Add the bulghur, reduce heat, and cook for 20 minutes, until the bulghur is soft and the water is absorbed. Set aside.

Preheat oven to 350 F. Heat the oil in a large skillet, over medium-high heat; add the onions and saute for 3 minutes. Add the beets, carrots, and cabbage, and saute for 7 minutes more. Add the seasonings. Remove from heat and combine with the bulghur.

Shape the batter into burgers to fit buns. Place on oiled cookie sheet, and bake for 10 minutes; turn over and bake for 10 minutes more.

CARROT BURGERS
Yields 1-1/2 dozen

10 carrots, peeled
  and cut into chunks
2 tablespoons oil
3 garlic cloves, minced
3 onions, cut into chunks
2 celery stalks, diced
2 green peppers, diced
5 tablespoons tamari
1/2 teaspoon garlic powder
1/2 teaspoon basil

1/2 teaspoon paprika
1/2 teaspoon oregano
1/2 teaspoon parsley
1/2 cup tahini
3 tablespoons peanut butter
2 tablespoons cashew butter
  (optional)
1/2 cup wheat germ,
  bran, or flour (optional)

Place the carrots in a medium-sized saucepan containing 3 or 4 inches of water; steam over medium heat for 15 minutes, till soft Drain and mash well using a potato masher.

In a large skillet, heat the oil over medium heat; add the diced garlic, onions, celery, and peppers; saute for 7 minutes. Add the tamari, basil, garlic powder, parsley, and oregano; saute for 2 minutes more, until vegetables are soft.

In a large bowl, combine the carrots, sauteed vegetables, tahini, and peanut butter. Season to taste. If the batter is too wet, add the wheat germ to make it hold together.

Preheat oven to 350 F. Form the mixture into patties, and place on an oiled cookie sheet. Bake for 10 to 12 minutes, until golden on top. Turn and bake on the other side until golden brown.

CAULIFLOWER PATTIES
Yields 2 dozen

2 large heads cauliflower
2 tablespoons oil
2 large onions, diced
1 stalk celery, diced
1 carrot, diced
2 garlic cloves, diced
4 tablespoons tamari

1/2 teaspoon sea salt
1/2 teaspoon oregano
1/2 teaspoon basil
1/2 teaspoon garlic powder
1/2 cup bran
1/4 cup flour
1/2 cup tahini or peanut butter

Cut cauliflower into quarters; place in a large pot with 2 cups water; steam over medium heat for 15 minutes, until soft. Drain, and mash with a potato masher.

Heat the oil in a skillet over medium heat; add the onions, celery, and carrots, and saute for 5 minutes, until brown. Add the diced garlic, and saute for 2 minutes more. Season to taste with the tamari, salt, oregano, basil, and garlic powder.

In a large bowl, combine the sauteed vegetables and the mashed cauliflower. Add the bran and flour to make the mixture hold together, adding more if needed. Add the tahini, and season to taste.

Preheat oven to 350 F. Oil a cookie sheet. Form the mixture into patties and place on the cookie sheet; bake for 10 minutes, or until golden brown on top. Turn over and bake for 10 minutes more.

VARIATION
Substitute broccoli for the cauliflower. Alter seasoning by adding sesame seeds, ground sunflower seeds, or nutritional yeast flakes.

MASHED POTATO PATTIES
Serves 4

6 large potatoes, cut into chunks
2 tablespoons oil
3 large onions, diced
1 carrot, diced
1 celery stalk, diced
1 pepper, diced
2 garlic cloves, diced
1/2 teaspoon oregano

1/2 teaspoon basil
1/2 teaspoon garlic powder
1/2 teaspoon sea salt
3 tablespoons tamari
3 tablespoons tahini
  or peanut butter
1/2 cup whole wheat flour

In a large pot, combine the potatoes with 5 cups water; place over medium heat and steam for 15 minutes, until soft.

Heat the oil in a large skillet over medium heat; add the onions, carrot, celery, and pepper, and saute for 7 minutes, until tender. Season with diced garlic, oregano, basil, garlic powder, sea salt, and tamari.

Drain the potatoes and mash well. Add the sauteed vegetables, tahini, and flour. Season to taste.

Preheat oven to 350 F. Oil 2 cookie sheets. Form the mixture into patties and place on the cookie sheets. Bake for 15 to 18 minutes, until crisp; turn over and bake for 15 minutes more.

EGGPLANT PATTIES
Yields 2 dozen

5 large eggplants, peeled
  and cut into chunks
2 tablespoons oil
3 garlic cloves, diced
3 large onions, diced
3 carrots, diced
2 stalks celery, diced
1 green pepper, diced

1/4 cup tamari
1/2 teaspoon basil
1/2 teaspoon garlic powder
1/2 teaspoon oregano
1/2 teaspoon paprika
1/2 cup tahini or peanut butter
2 tablespoons flour (optional)

In a large pot, combine the eggplant with 2 cups water; place over medium heat and steam for 5 minutes, until soft. Drain and mash well with a potato masher.

In a large skillet, heat the oil over medium heat; add the diced garlic, onions, carrots, celery, and pepper, and saute for 7 minutes. Season with the tamari, basil, and garlic powder.

In a large bowl, combine the eggplant, sauteed vegetables, and the remaining ingredients except the flour. Season to taste. If batter is too thin, add the flour.

Preheat oven to 350 F. Oil a cookie sheet. Form the mixture into patties and place on the sheet in even rows. Bake for 8 minutes, until golden on top. Turn over and bake for 8 minutes more.

POTATO LATKES
Yields 15 patties

5 to 7 large potatoes,
  grated and drained
1/2 cup soy powder
1 cup bran or flour
1 onion, grated
1/4 cup oil

4 tablespoons tamari
2 teaspoons garlic powder
1 teaspoon paprika
1 teaspoon sea salt
1/4 teaspoon basil

Combine all the ingredients in a large bowl. If the mixture is too loose, drain off more liquid or add more soy powder or flour.

Heat 2 tablespoons oil in a skillet over medium heat; drop the batter by the tablespoonful. Fry on each side for 7 minutes, until golden brown. Drain the patties on paper towel.

VARIATION

Add grated carrot to the mixture before forming patties.

SWEET POTATO PUFFS
Yields 2 dozen

10 sweet potatoes,
  peeled and cut into chunks
2 tablespoons oil
3 garlic cloves, diced
2 onions, cut into chunks
1 stalk celery, cut into chunks
2 peppers, diced
2 carrots, grated (optional)
1-1/2 teaspoons sea salt

1-1/2 cups cooked millet
5 tablespoons tahini,
  or peanut butter
3 tablespoons sesame seeds
1/3 cup tamari
1/2 teaspoon basil
1/2 teaspoon oregano
1/2 teaspoon garlic powder

Place the potatoes in a large pot with 3 cups of water, and steam for 15 minutes, until soft.

Heat the oil in a large skillet; add the diced garlic, onions, celery, peppers, and carrots. Saute for 7 minutes, until the vegetables are tender. Add all the seasonings.

Drain the potatoes and mash well. Add the millet, tahini, and the seasoned sauteed vegetables, and mix well.

Preheat oven to 350 F. Oil a cookie sheet. Drop the sweet potato mixture by the tablespoonful onto the sheet, being careful not to flatten the puffs. Sprinkle sesame seeds on top. Bake for 20 minutes.

VARIATION

Add wheat germ, bran, flour, or soy powder to the mixture with the millet.

MILLET BURGERS
Yields 3 dozen

3 cups millet
3 tablespoons oil
5 garlic cloves, diced
6 large onions, diced
3 stalks celery, diced
3 carrots, diced
1/3 cup tamari

1 teaspoon basil
1 teaspoon parsley
1 teaspoon garlic powder
1 teaspoon sea salt
1/2 teaspoon paprika
3 tablespoons peanut butter or tahini
1/2 cup wheat germ or bran

Bring 6 cups of water to a boil in a large pot; add the millet and cook over medium-low heat for 20 to 25 minutes, or until soft.

Heat the oil in a skillet over medium heat; add the garlic and onions, and saute for 3 minutes, until the onions are golden. Add the celery and carrots; cook for 4 minutes, until all the vegetables are tender.

Add the seasonings: 2 tablespoons tamari, 1/2 teaspoon each of parsley, basil, garlic powder, and sea salt; stir constantly. Remove from heat.

Preheat oven to 350 F. Oil cookie sheet. In a large bowl, combine the millet and the sauteed vegetables. Add the peanut butter, remaining tamari and remaining seasonings. Add wheat germ or bran to bind the mixture, and to reach a consistency that holds together.

Form the mixture into patties and place them on the cookie sheet. Bake for 15 minutes; turn over and bake for 15 minutes more, checking them periodically to prevent burning.

Great served in sandwiches.

ZUCCHINI SQUASH PATTIES
Yields 2 dozen

5 zucchini (or any other
  variety of summer squash)
2 tablespoons oil
4 garlic cloves, diced
4 large onions, diced
2 carrots, diced
2 stalks celery, diced
1 green pepper, diced
5 tablespoons tahini,
  or peanut butter

3 tablespoons tamari
1/2 teaspoon paprika
1/2 teaspoon oregano
1/2 teaspoon basil
1/2 teaspoon sea salt
1/8 teaspoon red pepper (optional)
1/2 cup sesame seeds
1/2 cup sunflower seed meal
1 cup corn meal,
  or flour, or soy powder

Slice the zucchini and place in a large pot with 1/2 cup water, adding enough squash to fill the pot. Steam over medium heat for 7 minutes, until soft.

Heat the oil in a large skillet over medium heat; add the garlic, onions, carrots, celery, and pepper; saute for 7 minutes, till vegetables are tender.

Drain the zucchini and mash well. Add the sauteed vegetables, tahini, seasonings, sesame seeds, sunflower seed meal, and corn meal. The batter should be thick, not wet—add flour if needed.

Preheat oven to 375 F. Oil a cookie sheet. Using a tablespoon, make patties and place them on the sheet. Bake for 8 minutes on each side, until golden brown.

RICE PATTIES
Yields 2 dozen

2 tablespoons oil
2 large onions, diced
1 stalk celery, diced
2 carrots, diced
1 green pepper, diced
2 garlic cloves, diced
6 tablespoons tamari

1/2 teaspoon garlic powder
1/2 teaspoon basil
1/2 teaspoon oregano
3 cups cooked rice
1/4 cup peanut butter
1/2 cup flour

In a large skillet, heat the oil over medium heat; add the onions and saute for 5 minutes, until golden.

Add the celery, carrots, and pepper; saute for 5 minutes, add the diced garlic, and saute for 5 minutes more until the vegetables are tender. Season with the tamari, garlic powder, basil and oregano.

Remove from heat. Add the rice. Season to taste. Add the peanut butter and flour.

Preheat oven to 350 F. Oil a cookie sheet. Form the mixture into patties, and place on the cookie sheet. Bake for 5 to 6 minutes until crispy golden on top; turn over and bake for 5 to 6 minutes more.

VARIATION

Substitute kasha (buckwheat groats), cous cous, or bulghur for the rice.

CHICK-PEA BURGERS
Yields 2 dozen

2 cups chick peas
6 cups water
2 tablespoons oil
2 garlic cloves, diced
2 large onions, diced
2 carrots, diced
3 stalks celery, diced
3 green peppers, diced
6 tablespoons tamari

1/2 teaspoon sea salt
1/2 teaspoon basil
1/4 teaspoon garlic powder
1/2 cup tahini,
  or peanut butter
  or cashew butter
1/4 teaspoon paprika
1/4 teaspoon oregano
1/4 teaspoon cumin

Soak the chick-peas in water to cover overnight.

Place chick peas in a pressure cooker with 6 cups water, and cook for 1 hour; or cook in a large pot for approximately 2 hours, until tender.

In a large skillet, heat the oil over medium heat; add the garlic, onions, carrots, celery, and peppers; saute for 7 minutes, until tender. Season with 3 tablespoons tamari, sea salt, basil, garlic powder.

Drain the chick-peas and mash well. Combine with the sauteed vegetables in a large bowl. Add the tahini and remaining seasonings.

The mixture should be mushy but light. If too thin, add some bran or whole wheat flour; if too thick, add some stock. Mix well.

Preheat oven to 350 F. Oil a cookie sheet. Form the mixture into patties and place on the sheet. Bake for 8 to 10 minutes, until golden brown on top; turn over and brown other side.

SOY BURGERS
Yields 2 dozen

2 cups soybeans
6 cups stock or water
2 tablespoons oil
4 garlic cloves, diced
2 large onions, diced
1 carrot, diced or grated
2 stalks celery, diced
1 green pepper, diced
1 teaspoon sea salt

1/2 teaspoon oregano
1/2 teaspoon garlic powder
1/2 teaspoon basil
1/2 teaspoon parsley
6 tablespoons tamari
2 tablespoons peanut butter
  or tahini (optional)
2 cups cooked millet,
  or cooked rice

Soak the soybeans in water to cover overnight.

Put soybeans and stock in a large pot, and cook over low heat for 2-1/2 hours until soft, making sure they are always covered with liquid.

Heat the oil in a large skillet over medium heat; add the garlic and saute for 3 or 4 minutes. Add the onions, and cook for 5 minutes, until golden. Mix in the carrots, celery, pepper, and seasonings. Cook for 2 minutes, until tender.

Preheat oven to 400 F. Oil a cookie sheet. Drain the soybeans and mash well. Combine with the sauteed vegetables and the millet in a large bowl. Add the tamari and peanut butter, if desired.

Form the mixture into patties and place on the cookie sheet. Bake for 20 minutes; turn burgers over and bake for 20 minutes more.

FALAFEL
Yields 2 dozen

2 cups chick-peas
5 cups stock or water
1/2 cup whole wheat flour
3 garlic cloves, diced

3 tablespoons parsley, chopped
1 tablespoon sea salt
1/4 teaspoon basil
3 to 5 cups oil (for deep frying)

Soak chick-peas in water to cover for 3 to 4 hours, or overnight.

Put chick peas and stock in a large pot, and cook for 1-1/2 to 2 hours, until soft; or cook in a pressure cooker for 1 hour.

Drain and mash well. Add the remaining ingredients, except the oil. The mixture will be medium hard. Form into 1-1/2" balls; roll in additional flour.

In a medium-size saucepan, over medium-high heat, heat the oil to 365 F. (test with a small drop of the mixture— it should sizzle). Deep fry the balls, 4 or 5 at a time, for 2 to 3 minutes, until light brown. Drain on paper towels. Serve with humus sauce (see recipe).

OKARA CYLINDERS
Yields 2-1/2 dozen

2 tablespoons oil
4 garlic cloves, diced fine
2 onions, diced fine
2 stalks celery, diced fine
1 carrot, grated
4 cups okara
3 potatoes, steamed and mashed
3 cups stock or water

3 tablespoons oil
3 tablespoons tamari
4 tablespoons tahini
1 teaspoon sea salt
1/4 teaspoon garlic powder
1/4 teaspoon basil
1/4 teaspoon oregano
1/2 to 1 cup whole wheat flour

Preheat oven to 350 F. Oil a cookie sheet. In a large skillet, heat the oil over medium-high heat; add the garlic and all the vegetables, and saute for 7 minutes until tender.

Place the okara in a large bowl; add the sauteed vegetables, potatoes, liquid, and remaining seasonings, stirring well. For a thicker batter add flour.

Shape the batter into cylinders or burgers; place on the cookie sheet. Bake for 7 or 8 minutes until golden; turn and cook for 7 or 8 minutes more.

"St. Francis considered all created beings as coming from the paternal heart of God. This community of origin made him feel a real fraternity with them all. He said: 'They have the same source as we had. Like us, they derive the life of thought, will and love from the Creator.

'.... Not to hurt our humble brethren was our first duty to them; but to stop there, a complete misapprehension of the intentions of Providence. We have a higher mission. God wishes that we succor them whenever they require it'."

St. Francis
(Quoted from St. Bonaventura)

"From an early age. I have abjured the use of meat, and the time will come when men will look upon the murder of animals as they look upon the murder of men."

Leonardo Da Vinci

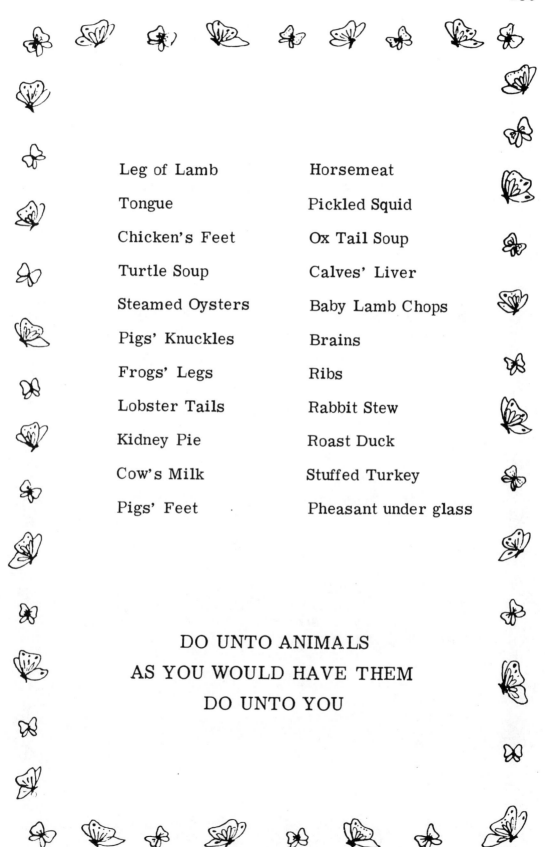

Leg of Lamb	Horsemeat
Tongue	Pickled Squid
Chicken's Feet	Ox Tail Soup
Turtle Soup	Calves' Liver
Steamed Oysters	Baby Lamb Chops
Pigs' Knuckles	Brains
Frogs' Legs	Ribs
Lobster Tails	Rabbit Stew
Kidney Pie	Roast Duck
Cow's Milk	Stuffed Turkey
Pigs' Feet	Pheasant under glass

DO UNTO ANIMALS
AS YOU WOULD HAVE THEM
DO UNTO YOU

"We should remember in our dealings with animals that they are a sacred trust to us from our Heavenly Father. They are dumb and cannot speak for themselves."

Harriet Beecher Stowe

"In the mountains of truth, you never climb in vain. Either you reach a higher point today, or you exercise your strength in order to be able to climb higher tomorrow."

Friedrich Wilhelm Nietzsche

Treats and Beverages

ROASTED COCONUT

Preheat oven to broil. Break outer shell off, and cut fresh coconut into slices. Peel thin brown skin off; place peeled slices on a cookie sheet. Broil until coconut turns golden brown; turn over and brown other side.

This roasted coconut is best if cooked over an open fire.

VARIATION

Grate the fresh coconut before placing it on cookie sheet and roasting. Turn grated coconut, to brown both sides.

BANANA COOKIES
Yields 2 dozen

3 ripe bananas, mashed
1/3 cup oil
3/4 cup sorghum
2 tablespoons soy powder
3 tablespoons water
   or orange juice

1 teaspoon vanilla
2-1/4 cups whole wheat
   pastry flour
1 teaspoon baking soda
1 teaspoon cinnamon
1/8 teaspoon sea salt

Preheat oven to 350 F. Oil a cookie sheet. In a large bowl, combine the bananas and all the liquid ingredients, mixing well.

In a separate bowl, combine all the dry ingredients; add to the liquid mixture, blending well into a thick batter.

Drop batter by teaspoonfuls onto the cookie sheet. Bake for 10 to 12 minutes, until golden.

OATMEAL CHEWIES
Yields 2 dozen

3 cups oats
1 cup whole wheat flour
1/2 teaspoon baking soda
1/3 cup oil
1/3 cup water
1 cup sorghum

1 teaspoon vanilla
2 teaspoons soy powder
1/2 to 1 cup raisins
1/4 teaspoon sea salt
Sprinkle of cinnamon

Preheat oven to 350 F. Oil a cookie sheet. In a large bowl, combine all the dry ingredients.

Blend together all the liquid ingredients in another large bowl; add the dry mixture.

Drop the batter by the teaspoonful onto the cookie sheet. Bake for 15 minutes.

PEANUT BUTTER COOKIES
Yields 2 dozen

3/4 cup peanut butter
1/2 cup sweetener (sorghum)
1/4 cup date sugar
1/3 cup oil

1/4 teaspoon sea salt
1 teaspoon vanilla
1 cup whole wheat pastry flour

Preheat oven to 350 F. Oil a cookie sheet. In a large bowl, combine all the ingredients except the flour. Gradually mix the flour in.

Drop batter by teaspoonfuls, onto the cookie sheet; flatten each cookie with a fork. Bake for 8 to 10 minutes.

VARIATION

Add chopped nuts or raisins to the batter.

VANILLA COOKIES
Yields 2 dozen

1/2 cup oil
1/2 cup sorghum
1 tablespoon soy powder
   and 2 tablespoons water
1 tablespoon vanilla

1-1/4 cups whole wheat pastry flour
1/8 cup soy powder
1/2 teaspoon baking soda
1/4 cup chopped nuts (optional)

Preheat oven to 400 F. Oil a cookie sheet. In a large bowl, cream together the oil, sorghum, soy powder mix, and vanilla.

In a separate bowl, combine all the dry ingredients; add to the liquid, mixing well to form a smooth batter.

Drop the batter by teaspoonfuls onto the cookie sheet. Bake for 8 to 10 minutes.

LIGHT RAISIN COOKIES
Yields 3 dozen

1 cup water
2 cups raisins
2/3 cup oil
1-1/2 cups sorghum
4 tablespoons soy powder
   and 1/3 cup water
3 teaspoons vanilla
4 cups whole wheat pastry flour

1 teaspoon baking soda
2 teaspoons cinnamon
1 teaspoon sea salt
1/4 teaspoon nutmeg
1/4 teaspoon allspice
1 cup chopped nuts
1 cup wheat germ

Preheat oven to 350 F. Oil a cookie sheet. Put the water and raisins in a small saucepan, and simmer over low heat for 5 minutes; cool.

In a large bowl, combine the oil, sorghum, and the soy powder mixture (it should be creamy); add the vanilla, mixing well. Stir in the raisin mixture and the remaining ingredients, adding just enough wheat germ to make a teaspoon of batter hold its shape.

Drop the batter, by the teaspoonful, onto the cookie sheet. Bake for 8 to 10 minutes. Cool and serve.

OATMEAL COOKIES
Yields 5 dozen

3/4 cup oil
1 cup date sugar
3/4 cup sorghum
1/3 cup soymilk
2 teaspoons vanilla
2-1/2 cups flour

1/2 teaspoon baking soda
1 teaspoon sea salt
3 cups rolled oats
1/2 cup raisins
3/4 teaspoon cinnamon

Add oil, sweetener, soy milk, and vanilla together, and beat until smooth. Add remaining ingredients and mix well.

Bake at 350 F. for about 10 minutes, or until the undersides just start turning brown.

CAROB COOKIES
Yields 4 dozen

2-1/4 cups whole wheat pastry flour
6 tablespoons carob powder
1/2 teaspoon baking soda
1/2 cup mixed raisins
and nuts, chopped

2/3 cup oil
1-1/4 cup sorghum
2 teaspoons vanilla
1-1/2 tablespoons soy powder
and 3 tablespoons water

Preheat oven to 400 F. Oil a cookie sheet. Combine all the dry ingredients in a large bowl. Mix together all the liquid ingredients in another large bowl; add the dry mixture, 1/3 at a time, mixing well.

Drop the batter by the tablespoonful onto the cookie sheet, allowing 1/2'' between cookies. Bake for 8 to 10 minutes.

CAROB BROWNIES
Yields 1 dozen

1/2 cup oil
1/3 cup sorghum
1/3 cup date sugar
2 tablespoons soy powder
and 4 tablespoons water
1 teaspoon vanilla
1/2 teaspoon sea salt

1/2 cup carob powder
2/3 cup whole wheat pastry flour
1 teaspoon baking soda
1/2 cup mixed nuts
and raisins, chopped
3 tablespoons soy milk

Preheat oven to 375 F. Oil a 9'' square baking pan. In a large bowl, combine the oil, sweeteners, soy powder mixture, and vanilla.

In a separate bowl, combine the sea salt, carob powder, flour, baking soda, and nuts and raisins; add to the liquid mixture. Add the soymilk and mix well.

Transfer batter to the baking pan and bake for 30 minutes; cut into squares while still warm.

CAROB CAKE
Yields 2 8-inch round cakes

1/2 cup oil or margarine
1/2 cup date sugar
1/2 cup sorghum
4 tablespoons soy powder
  and 6 tablespoons water
1/2 cup carob powder
  and 1/2 cup water

1-1/2 teaspoons vanilla
3 cups whole wheat pastry flour
1 teaspoon baking soda
1 teaspoon Postum
1/2 cup mixed nuts
  and raisins, chopped
3/4 cup thick nut milk (see recipe)

Preheat oven to 350 F. Oil two 8'' baking pans. In a large bowl, combine the oil, date sugar, and sorghum; mix together the soy powder and 6 tablespoons water, and add this to the mixture.

Combine the carob and 1/2 cup of water; add to the mixture. Add vanilla. In a separate bowl, combine the flour, soda, Postum, and nuts and raisins; add to the liquid mixture. Mix in the thick nut milk.

Divide the batter equally between the pans; bake for 30 to 35 minutes, testing by sticking a toothpick in the center of cake—if it comes out dry, the cake is done.

VARIATION

For vanilla cake, omit the carob, and add 3 teaspoons more vanilla and 1/2 cup more flour.

TOFU CHEESECAKE
Yields 1 pie

Crust

2 cups whole wheat pastry flour
1/4 cup date sugar
1/4 teaspoon salt
1/2 teaspoon cinnamon

1/3 cup oil
2 tablespoons water
1/4 cup sorghum

Preheat oven to 350 F. Mix dry ingredients together. Add oil, water, and sorghum, and work with your fingers. Pat on bottom and half-way up the sides of a 9'' pie plate.

Partially bake for 10 minutes, before adding filling for final baking. (For a completely prebaked shell—used in other recipes—bake for 15 minutes.)

Filling

3 cups tofu
1/3 cup fresh lemon juice
1/3 cup oil
1 cup date sugar

3/4 teaspoon salt
1-1/4 teaspoon vanilla
1/2 cup raisins (optional)

Combine ingredients in a blender; blend at high speed for 1 minute. Mixture should be a thick, creamy consistency.

Pour into partially baked crust, and bake for half hour.

APPLESAUCE CAKE
Serves 6 to 8

1/2 cup oil
1 cup date sugar
1/2 cup sorghum
1-1/2 cups unsweetened
   applesauce
2 cups whole wheat pastry flour

1/2 teaspoon sea salt
1/2 teaspoon baking soda
1 teaspoon cinnamon
1/4 teaspoon ginger
1/2 teaspoon allspice
1/8 teaspoon nutmeg

Mix oil and sweetener well; add applesauce, and mix the dry ingredients in. Beat until smooth. Pour into an oiled and floured 8-inch cake pan, and bake at 350 F. for 45 minutes.

DANISH
Yields 2 loaves

2 tablespoons dry active yeast
1/3 cup & 1 tablespoon date sugar
1/2 cup lukewarm water
1/2 cup sorghum
3/4 cup thick soymilk
   (6 tablespoons soy powder
   and 1/2 cup water)
1 teaspoon sea salt
1/2 cup oil

1 teaspoon lemon rind, grated
1/2 cup hot water
4-3/4 cups whole wheat
   pastry flour, sifted
1/3 cup additional date sugar
2 tablespoons cinnamon
2 teaspoons nutmeg
1 cup nuts and raisins, chopped, or
   1 cup applesauce or prune whip

In a small bowl, combine the yeast, 1 tablespoon date sugar, and the warm water.

In a large bowl, combine the 1/3 cup date sugar, sorghum, soymilk, sea salt, oil, lemon rind, and the hot water; and mix well. Add the yeast mixture. Gradually add the sifted flour in 4 parts, mixing well each time. Cover and allow to rise for 20 minutes.

Turn dough onto a well floured board and knead for approximately 10 minutes until satiny smooth, adding flour as needed.

Place in an oiled bowl; oil the top of the dough. Cover and allow to rise for approximately 1 hour, until doubled in bulk. Punch the dough down.

Divide the dough in half; roll out one half on a floured board, to a 9'' x 12'' rectangle. Cover with a layer of 2 tablespoons oil. Sprinkle with half the amounts of date sugar, cinnamon, nutmeg, chopped raisins and nuts (or applesauce or prune whip).

Roll up like a jelly roll; pinch ends. Place on oiled cookie sheet. Repeat for other half of dough. Allow to rise approximately 1 hour, till doubled in bulk.

Preheat oven to 325 F. Bake for 20 to 30 minutes, watching carefully to prevent burning.

Danish Glaze

3 tablespoons sorghum
3 tablespoons oil

1 tablespoon date sugar
1/4 cup chopped nuts

Combine sorghum, oil, and date sugar in a saucepan; bring to a boil over medium heat. Spread the hot glaze over the hot Danish. Sprinkle with chopped nuts.

BANANA BREAD
Yields 1 loaf

1/2 cup date sugar
1/2 cup sorghum
1/2 cup safflower oil
2 tablespoons soy powder
  and 3 tablespoons water
3 ripe bananas, mashed

2-1/2 cups whole wheat flour
1 teaspoon baking soda
1/2 teaspoon cinnamon
1/2 cup walnuts, chopped
1/2 cup raisins, chopped

Preheat oven to 350 F. Oil a loaf pan. In a large bowl, combine the sweeteners, oil, and soy mixture, mixing until smooth. Add the mashed bananas.
  In a separate bowl, combine all the dry ingredients; add to the liquid.
  Transfer mixture to a loaf pan or 9'' cake pan. Bake for 1 hour; test with a toothpick in the middle— if still wet, reduce oven to 300 F. and bake for 15 minutes more.

BANANA CREAM PIE
Yields 1 9-inch pie

2 to 3 ripe bananas
1 teaspoon vanilla
1 tablespoon lemon juice
1/2 cup oil

1 cup date sugar
1/4 cup sorghum
1/4 teaspoon sea salt
2-1/2 cups tofu

Blend all ingredients in a blender until creamy and smooth. Pour the thick creamy blend into a prebaked pie shell, and chill for 3 to 4 hours. Use pie crust recipe from Tofu Cheesecake.

CAROB TOFU CREAM PIE
Yields 1 9-inch pie

3 cups tofu
3/4 cup oil
1 cup date sugar
1/2 cup sorghum

3/4 cup carob
2 teaspoons vanilla
1/4 teaspoon sea salt
1/2 cup water

Blend ingredients, using the water to help blend the tofu. Try to blend as thick a cream as possible, so it will set nicely when refrigerated. Pour into prebaked pie shell (see Tofu Cheesecake pie crust recipe), and refrigerate for a couple of hours.

PIE CRUST
Yields 2 crusts for a 9" pie

1-3/4 cups whole wheat pastry flour
1/4 cup soy powder
1/4 cup cold orange juice

1/2 cup oil
1 teaspoon vanilla

Combine the flour and soy powder in a medium sized bowl, and mix thoroughly. In a large bowl, combine the liquid ingredients, mixing vigorously until completely blended. Add the dry mixture; mix for 4 minutes, until dough is soft.

It is best to use the dough immediately, as it is then easiest to roll out. Pre-heat oven to 350 F. Place a sheet of waxed paper on a slightly dampened counter (the dampness keeps the waxed paper in place and prevents it from wrinkling). Sprinkle waxed paper with flour.

Take a little more than half of the dough and form it into a ball. Place it on the waxed paper and roll it thin, to make a round crust to fit a 9" pie plate.

Pick up waxed paper with the pastry on it and turn it over into pie plate. Peel waxed paper off. Press pastry into place, and fill it with pie filling (see below).

Use the rest of the dough in the same way, to make top crust. Place over the filling; trim excess pastry around the edge, and press edges of crusts together. Make a few fork holes in top pie-crust.

Bake at 350 F. for about 40 minutes.

APPLE PIE FILLING
Yields 1 pie

5 medium size apples
 (preferably Rome Beauty)
1/4 cup sorghum

2 teaspoons cinnamon
1/4 teaspoon nutmeg
1 tablespoon date sugar

Peel and core the apples, cut into bite-size pieces, and place in a large bowl. Pour the sorghum over the apples, stirring constantly to assure even sweetness. Sprinkle with cinnamon and nutmeg, and mix thoroughly. Sprinkle with date sugar. Add sweetener to taste.

CRUMB PIE TOPPING

1/2 cup oil
1/4 cup ice cold juice or water
1/3 cup sorghum
1/4 cup date sugar

2 cups whole wheat pastry flour
1 teaspoon cinnamon
1/2 teaspoon nutmeg

Preheat oven to 300 F. Mix together in a bowl: date sugar, flour, cinnamon, and nutmeg. In a separate bowl, mix the oil, juice, and sorghum. Add the dry ingredients to the liquid mixture, and mix well. Crumble into bite-size pieces onto a baking sheet. Bake for 20 minutes, turning twice.

FRUIT PASTRY
Yields 4 loaves

1 cup oil
1 cup sorghum
1 teaspoon vanilla
Grated rind of 1 orange or lemon
5 to 6 tablespoons soy powder
   and 1/2 cup water

4 cups whole wheat pastry flour
1 teaspoon baking soda
1-1/2 cups applesauce,
   or strawberry preserve,
   or blueberry preserve

In a large bowl, combine the oil, sorghum, vanilla, and grated rind. Mix the soy powder and water together till thick and creamy, and stir into the liquid mixture.

In a separate bowl, combine the flour and baking soda; add to the liquid mixture, stirring until batter doesn't stick to the fingers. If too dry, add a little oil. Chill batter for 3 to 4 hours.

Preheat oven to 350 F. Oil 2 cookie sheets.

Divide the dough into 4 equal parts. Roll one part out on floured wax paper, rolling from the center out. Place 3 to 4 tablespoons of appplesauce or preserves on the strip of dough. Roll the dough up lengthwise; pinch the ends to prevent filling from oozing out.

Remove from wax paper, and place on the cookie sheet. Prepare remaining loaves. Bake for 25 to 30 minutes. Cut into slices while hot; cool before serving.

VARIATION

For filling: raisins, chopped dates, shredded coconut, chopped nuts.

FROZEN BANANAS

Peel ripe bananas and freeze in plastic bags. Slice each frozen banana thin, and serve with nut or fruit topping.

If desired, roll whole frozen banana in peanut butter, or carob candy butter, or carob syrup, coating thoroughly; then in granola, crushed nuts, or shredded coconut.

Return to freezer.

BANANA ICE CREAM

1 ripe banana per bowl

Peel and freeze the banana. Put the frozen banana through a Champion Juicer set up to homogenize, or through any appliance that homogenizes.

BANANA FUDGE ICE CREAM
Serves 2

1/2 cup frozen carob candy   3 peeled frozen bananas
   (see recipe)

Place 1 frozen banana and 1 chunk of carob candy in a Champion juicer set to homogenize. Repeat until all bananas are processed.

VARIATION

Substitute peanut butter or frozen fruit (instead of the candy) to make the fudge. Put 1 tablespoon peanut butter through the juicer, followed by a frozen banana.

VANILLA ICE CREAM
Serves 3

3 bananas   4 tablespoons soy powder
4 tablespoons cashew butter   1 teaspoon vanilla
1/2 cup sorghum   1 tablespoon slippery elm powder
2 cups water   1/4 teaspoon sea salt

Combine all the ingredients in a blender and blend at high speed for 1 minute. Transfer to an ice cream maker, and process for 1-1/2 hours. For a large machine, double the recipe.

VARIATION

Freeze the blended mix, cut into chunks, and serve.

CAROB ICE CREAM
Serves 4

2 cups water   4 tablespoons peanut butter
1 teaspoon vanilla   or cashew butter
1/2 cup sorghum   1/8 cup date sugar
3 or 4 bananas   1 tablespoon soy powder
3 heaping tablespoons   1 tablespoon slippery elm powder
   carob powder

Place all ingredients (liquids first) in a blender, and blend well at high speed. Transfer to an ice cream maker, and process for 1-1/2 hours. Or: freeze the blended mix; when ready to serve, reblend with another banana or cut into chunks.

RICH NUT ICE CREAM
Serves 4

1 cup soymilk
1/2 cup almonds
1/2 cup cashews
1/2 cup sunflower seeds

1/2 cup sesame seeds
1/4 cup sorghum
2 tablespoons oil
1/2 teaspoon vanilla

Put all ingredients in blender, and blend at high speed for 1 minute. Put into a large bowl, individual bowls, or a tray. Cover and freeze. When frozen, cut into chunks and serve.

VARIATION

Use 2 cups of assorted raw nuts in place of the almonds, cashews, and sunflower seeds.

SHERBET
Yields 1 quart

2 cups orange juice
2 ripe bananas, sliced
1/4 cup sweetener

1 cup pitted fruit (strawberry, cherry, raisin, peach, apple, etc.)

Combine all the ingredients in a blender; blend at high speed for 1 minute, until smooth. Pour into a large plastic container or small individual cups; freeze to desired consistency. Serve plain, or garnished with fresh fruit.

BANANA ORANGE FREEZE
Serves 2

2 cups orange juice   2 bananas, sliced

Pour the juice into a shallow plastic container. Drop banana slices on top. Cover and freeze. Serve as sherbet-type treat.

VARIATION

Sprinkle shredded coconut on top before freezing.

FUDGESICLES
Yields 1 quart

2-1/2 cups water
1/2 cup sorghum
3 bananas, fresh or frozen, sliced
1/2 cup carob powder

1 tablespoon slippery elm powder
1 tablespoon vanilla
5 tablespoons peanut butter

Blend all the ingredients at medium speed for 1 minute, until you have a smooth, medium-thick syrup. Pour into a plastic container, or individual cups; freeze overnight.

HOT FUDGE TOPPING
Yields 2 cups

1-1/2 cups water
1 teaspoon vanilla
4 tablespoons sorghum
3 tablespoons soy powder

2 tablespoons peanut butter
6 tablespoons carob powder
1 teaspoon Postum

Combine all the ingredients in the order given; mix until creamy. Serve hot or cold.

NUT TOPPING
Yields 1 cup

1 cup sunflower seeds,
    cashews, or almonds

Place 2 tablespoons of the seeds or nuts in a blender and blend for 30 seconds until crunchy. Repeat until all are blended.
    Use as a topping for ice cream, pastry, or salad; or add to casseroles.

VARIATION

Roast the seeds before blending.

CAROB FROSTING
Yields 2 cups

1/2 cup carob powder
1/2 cup date sugar
1/8 cup sorghum
2 tablespoons peanut
    or cashew butter

1 tablespoon soy powder
1 teaspoon Postum
1 teaspoon vanilla
1/4 cup-oil, or 3 bananas, mashed
1/4 cup water

Put all the ingredients in a blender, and blend at high speed for 1 minute, till thick and creamy. Chill in refrigerator until ready to be served. Serve over ice cream or cake.

CAROB SAUCE
Yields 3 cups

1-1/2 cups water
1 teaspoon vanilla
3 tablespoons sorghum
1 frozen banana

1/2 ripe banana
6 tablespoons carob powder
1 tablespoon soy powder
1/2 cup peanut butter

Place the liquid ingredients in a blender, and blend for 30 seconds at medium speed; add the remaining ingredients and blend for 30 seconds more. To thin, add more liquid; to thicken, add additional peanut butter or frozen bananas. To sweeten, add more sorghum.

CAROB BALLS
Yields 2 dozen

1/2 cup carob powder
1/3 cup soy powder
1/2 cup sunflower seeds, chopped
1/2 cup raisins, chopped

1/2 cup sorghum
1/4 cup safflower oil
1/4 cup water
1 teaspoon vanilla

In a medium sized bowl, combine the carob, soy powder, sunflower seeds, and raisins. In a large bowl, combine the sorghum, oil, water, and vanilla; add the dry mixture and mix well. Roll the dough into small balls and chill.
Before serving, roll the balls in shredded coconut, if desired.

CAROB CANDY
Yields 1 8-inch tray

1/2 cup carob
2/3 cup nuts, chopped
1/2 cup raisins, chopped
1/2 cup shredded coconut
2 tablespoons date sugar

1/2 cup sorghum
3 tablespoons peanut butter
1 tablespoon vanilla
3 tablespoons soy powder
  and 5 tablespoons water

Combine all the dry ingredients in a bowl; combine all the liquid ingredients in a large bowl. Add the dry mixture to the liquid. If batter is too thick gradually add water until creamy. Put mixture in freezing tray, and freeze.

CAROB FUDGE
Yields 3 8-inch trays

1-1/2 cups carob powder
1/2 cup sunflower seeds, chopped
1/2 cup raisins, chopped
1-1/2 cups water

1/2 cup sorghum
1 cup peanut butter
1 tablespoon vanilla

Combine the carob powder, seeds, and raisins in a large bowl. In a separate bowl, combine the remaining ingredients; add dry ingredients to the liquid, and stir well until creamy.
Spoon into a shallow dish or tray and cover. Freeze overnight.

CAROB PUDDING
Yields 4 to 6 cups

4 cups nut milk, (see recipe)
1/4 cup date sugar and
  1/4 cup sorghum, or
  1/2 cup sorghum

1/3 cup carob powder
6 tablespoons arrowroot powder
1 teaspoon vanilla
1 teaspoon Postum

Combine all the ingredients in a blender; blend at high speed for 1 minute. Put mixture in a large saucepan; cook over low heat, stirring constantly, for 7 to 10 minutes, until thick. Transfer to cups and chill.

FRUIT SOUP
Serves 4 to 6

1 pound cherries, pitted
1/2 pound plums, pitted and sliced
1/2 pound peaches, pitted and sliced
1/2 cup raisins

3 cups water
2 tablespoons sweetener, if desired
1 tablespoon soy powder

In a large soup pot, combine the fruit, raisins, and water. Cook over medium heat for 10 minutes, stirring occasionally.

Add the sweetener, if desired; dilute the soy powder in one cup of the fruit liquid and mix into the soup. Cook for 5 minutes more.

Allow to sit for an hour or more before serving, if desired. Very good served cold.

VARIATION

Substitute other fruits (such as seedless grapes, nectarines, and pears) for the cherries, plums, and peaches.

BANANA SMOOTHIE
Yields 2-1/2 cups

1 frozen banana, sliced
1/2 banana, sliced

2 cups orange juice

Combine all the ingredients in a blender and blend at high speed for 1 minute, until creamy.

To thicken, add more banana.

FLAXSEED SMOOTHIE
Yields about 2 cups

1/4 cup flaxseed
1 cup water

1/2 banana, sliced
1/2 frozen banana, sliced

Soak the flaxseed overnight in water to cover.

In a blender, combine the flaxseed, water, banana, and frozen banana, and blend at high speed for 1 minute.

To thicken, add more banana. Good also as a laxative.

VARIATION

Substitute any fruit juice for the water.

To use flaxseed only as a laxative, soak 2 teaspoons of flaxseed in 4 tablespoons of liquid overnight. Eat as is.

CHERRY SMOOTHIE
Serves 2 or 3

5 cups of pitted watermelon
2 frozen bananas, sliced

1/2 cup pitted cherries
1/2 ripe banana, sliced

Place all ingredients in a blender and blend at high speed for 1 minute. If too thick, add water or watermelon; if too thin, add more frozen banana.

VARIATION

Add 2 cups apple juice, orange juice, or any other fruit juice, instead of the watermelon.
Add frozen strawberries, papaya, peaches, pineapple.

BLACK CHERRY FLOAT
(A float is a smoothie topped with banana ice cream)

5 cups watermelon, pitted
1 ripe banana, sliced
2 frozen bananas, sliced

1/2 cup frozen cherries, pitted
1/2 cup orange juice (optional)

Place the seeded watermelon in a blender, and blend at medium speed for 30 seconds; blend until it becomes juice. Combine 2 cups of this juice with the remaining ingredients. To thicken, add more frozen banana; to thin, add more liquid.
Pour smoothie into a tall glass; top with banana ice cream, and serve.

VARIATION

Substitute any other fruit juice for the watermelon juice.

POSTUM WHIP
Yields 2 cups

2 cups water
2 teaspoons Postum

2 heaping teaspoons soy powder
2 teaspoons sorghum

In a saucepan, heat the water to a boil; transfer to a blender. Add the Postum, soy powder, and sorghum; blend at medium speed for 30 seconds. Serve hot.
An excellent coffee substitute.

HOT COCOA WHIP
Yields 3 cups

2-1/2 cups water
2 teaspoons Postum
2 teaspoons carob powder
2 teaspoons soy powder

2 teaspoons sorghum
1/2 teaspoon slippery elm powder
   (optional)

In a saucepan, heat the water to a boil; combine with the remaining ingredients in a blender, and blend at medium speed for 30 seconds. Serve hot.

HOT SLIPPERY ELM WHIP
Health Reviver
Yields 2 cups

(This is an herbal medicine for calming and relaxing the stomach. It gives a protective coating and is excellent for stomach ache.)

1-1/2 cups water
1 teaspoon slippery elm powder

1 teaspoon soy powder
1 teaspoon sorghum

In a saucepan, heat the water until boiling, combine with remaining ingredients in a blender. Blend at medium-high speed for 1 minute. Serve hot.

VARIATION

Substitute peppermint, chamomile, or any herbal tea drink for the water.

COLD SLIPPERY ELM DRINK

1-1/2 cups cold water
1 teaspoon slippery elm powder

1/2 frozen banana, sliced
1 teaspoon sweetener, (optional)

Combine all the ingredients in a blender. Blend at high speed for 30 seconds.

HOT APPLE DRINK
Yields 2 cups

2 cups apple juice
1 cinnamon stick

Sprinkle of cinnamon

In a saucepan, combine all the ingredients and heat; serve hot.

CAROB MALTED
Yields 1 quart

2 cups water
3 frozen bananas, sliced
2 tablespoons carob powder
1/2 teaspoon vanilla

1 tablespoon sorghum
2 tablespoons peanut butter
1 tablespoon tahini (optional)

Combine all the ingredients in a blender; blend at high speed for 1 minute, and serve.

TAHINI BANANA MALTED
Yields 3 cups

2 cups water
2 frozen bananas, sliced

1-1/2 tablespoons tahini
1 teaspoon vanilla

Combine all the ingredients in a blender; blend at high speed for 1 minute, until creamy and smooth. If too thick, add water; if too thin, add more frozen banana.

Tastes like a vanilla thick shake.

VEGETABLE JUICE COCKTAIL
Yields 1-1/2 cups

1 cup carrot juice
1/4 cup spinach juice
1/4 cup red pepper juice
1/4 cup celery juice

1/8 cup beet juice
1/8 cup comfrey juice
1 tablespoon nutritional yeast

Add all ingredients to blender. Blend at medium speed for 30 seconds. Serve with a squeeze of lemon.

WHEAT GRASS JUICE
Yields 2 cups

2 cups wheatgrass

2 cups water

Combine the cut wheat grass with 2 cups of water and blend at medium speed for 1 minute; strain and pour into a jar. Keep refrigerated. It is best to use it the first day, when fresh.

LIME RICKEY
or
WHEATGRASS ORANGE JUICE COCKTAIL
Serves 2

2 cups wheatgrass juice   1/4 fresh lime or lemon
3/4 cup orange juice

Combine the wheatgrass juice with the orange juice. Squeeze the juice from a lime; add ice, and shake well, or blend in blender. A refreshing drink.

GRASSHOPPER
Yields 2 8-ounce glassfuls

3 cups frozen orange juice   1/4 cup orange juice
1/4 cup wheatgrass juice,   1 slice of lemon
   (see recipe)

Using a pestle, crush frozen orange juice. Place into 2 large glasses. Add the wheatgrass juice and the orange juice. Top with lemon slice.

PORANGE PUNCH
Yields 2 cups

1 cup peach stock   1 cup fresh orange juice
   (from cooking fresh peaches)
   or 1 cup fresh peach juice

Mix, and serve over ice.

ORANGE CRUSH
Yields 2 8-ounce glassfuls

3 cups frozen orange juice   1 cup fresh orange juice

Using a pestle, crush frozen orange juice. Place in 2 large glasses. Add the fresh orange juice.
Delicious on a hot day.

ANIMAL RIGHTS MARCH

(Sung to the tune, "Battle Hymn of the Republic")

Our eyes have seen the suffering the animals go through
Our eyes have seen the suffering the animals go through
Our eyes have seen the suffering the animals go through
They do have feelings, too.

We'll keep marching 'til they're all free
We'll keep marching 'til they're all free
We'll keep marching 'til they're all free
The truth is on our side.

You cannot cure the human race if love's not in your heart
You cannot cure the human race if love's not in your heart
You cannot cure the human race if love's not in your heart
Love's where you have to start.

We'll keep marching 'til they're all free
We'll keep marching 'til they're all free
We'll keep marching 'til they're all free
The truth is on our side.

God gave life to the animals just like he gave to you
God gave life to the animals just like he gave to you
God gave life to the animals just like he gave to you
This world is their world, too.

We'll keep marching 'til they're all free
We'll keep marching 'til they're all free
We'll keep marching 'til they're all free
The truth is on our side.

Light

"To a man whose mind is free, there is something more intolerable in the suffering of animals than in the suffering of men. For with the latter, it is at least admitted that suffering is evil and that the man who causes it is a criminal. But thousands of animals are uselessly butchered every day without a shadow of remorse. If any man were to refer to it, he would be thought ridiculous. And that is the unpardonable crime. That alone is the justification of all that men may suffer. It cries vengeance upon all the human race. If God exists and tolerates it, it cries vengeance upon God. If there exists a good God, then even the most humble of living things must be saved. If God is good only to the strong, if there is no justice for the weak and lowly, for the poor creatures who are offered up as a sacrifice to humanity, then there is no such thing as goodness, no such thing as justice...."

Romain Rolland
("Jean Christophe")

SIGNS of the TIMES

250 Marching Youngsters Protest Killing of Animals

Ground Bone in Meat Products Called Peril by Nutrition Experts

Swiss Offers $400,000 to 'Buy Lives' of 170,000 Baby Seals

Some of the Young Kill on shelf

Sorry, Dear. Meat's off!

Meat 8 months old?

VEGETARIANISM FOR A WORLD OF PLENTY

Ethics, not health

Meat, Fish Much To Bear

Fall from Grace

Cancer-Causing Chemicals in Meat

Killing of Too Many Animals Deplored

Showing Animals

Fur They're Killing Our Horses For Meat

Norway to curb meat consumption

Growing Way of Life

Good case for vegetarian diet

now for vegetarian

Singer turns vegetarian

Pity the Poor Mink, Not the Rich

CASE NO. 3 CATS TRAPPED ON TREADMILLS

LABS TORTURE ANIMALS?

Meat Can Be Risky, Nutritionist Says

Vegetarianism

Kicked the Meat Habit

Frank's 'Bunny Bill' hops hurdle

animal cruelty is admitted

Vegetables for moral reasons

Must Thousands Of Rabbits Suffer To Produce Another Mascara?

Food For The Traveling Vegan

Anyone "on the road" who wishes to avoid fast-food (fat food) restaurants, should travel with a "food box" of various staple items in convenient containers. Here is a list of suggested items for vegans:

1. NUT AND FRUIT MIX— Any combination of nuts, seeds, raisins, dried fruit, coconut, etc.

2. PEANUT BUTTER.

3. TAHINI— Mix with water and tamari to make salad dressing, or to spread on bread.

4. TAMARI (or salt substitute)— Use on sandwiches, vegetables, etc.

5. NUTRITIONAL YEAST— Mix in salad dressings, or sprinkle over food.

6. TOFU— Store under water, in sealed container. Use sliced and seasoned,or mashed as a spread for sandwiches.

7. WHOLE-GRAIN BREADS— Sliced whole-wheat, pita "pocket" bread, or rice cakes; all are convenient on the road. Sandwich ideas: guacamole (avocado dip), tofu "eggless" salad, peanut butter with banana or fruit spread, etc.

8. CEREALS— For breakfast: granola, puffed or flaked whole-grains, etc. Top with fresh fruit, and use soy milk (Edensoy, Ah Soy), bottled nut milk or fruit juice, etc., instead of dairy milk.

9. Fresh drinking water.

10. If on an extended trip, some shopping may be necessary for fresh produce: lettuce, tomato, onion, sprouts, fruits, etc.

11. NECESSARY UTENSILS— Such as plates, bowls, cups, napkins, spoons, forks and knives (including paring/cutting knife), cutting tray, peeler.

For convenience in traveling, keep tahini and tamari in plastic squeeze-bottles, and nutritional yeast in a small container with a secure lid.

If you go to a restaurant, eat from the salad bar, and look for menu items featuring pastas, and side-dish selections of vegetables. Inform the waiter that you are interested in meatless entrees, and he may know of a special dish that the chef can prepare for you. Beware of cream sauces, and other dairy-containing condiments in salad dressings, dessert toppings, etc.

Recipes for Dogs and Cats

FOOD FOR YOUR PET

Dogs, contrary to popular belief, are not obligated to be meat eaters. Their nutritional requirements are essentially the same as yours, and your dog should thrive on the same excellent nutrition that you receive through the food in this book. We have seen our dogs stay sleek and healthy and their coats grow rich and glossy, from eating vegan food.

If your dog is still eating commercial dog food, start by preparing selections from the following recipes and mix them into the present food, gradually increasing the proportion of vegetarian food and decreasing the amount of meat. Soon your dog will become leaner, healthier, and gentler before your eyes. Green and yellow vegetables cooked and blended into the grain mixture supply essential vitamins and minerals. Of course, the leftovers from your table, including tofu, sprouts, avocados, etc., can and should be added to your dog's meal. Commercial vegan dog food, fortified with vitamins, is available, and a small amount of this may be added to each feeding to assure adequate vitamin intake, especially for puppies.

Our dogs, Magic and Miracles, have been bright and happy on a vegan diet for years. Miracles has been raised as a vegan dog from birth and recommends "Vegetable Medley For Puppies", while Magic loves tofu chunks and whole wheat bread or crackers added to her meals.

The recipes presented here are well liked by dogs and cats, are easy to prepare, and should form the foundation of your pet's diet. Cats present a special situation because, unlike dogs and humans, they seem unable to manufacture an amino acid "protein building block" called taurine. When deprived of taurine, kittens do not grow and thrive, and may suffer damage to the retinas of their eyes. At this time, no practical plant source of taurine is available. However, a bright hope for cats and their human friends seems to have emerged in the form of "Vegecat", a non-animal taurine/vitamin supplement, now commercially available. Apparently, this product added to a balanced vegan diet (which should include soaked and sprouted legumes, seeds, and grains) will keep cats healthy.

The pet foods created in the following recipes are less expensive than commercial products, and untainted by the violence of the slaughterhouse. A diet without meat is not only nutritionally sound for dogs and now cats, it helps them evolve into gentler, healthier pets.

HINTS FOR FEEDING

1. Add chunks of bread to the meal.

2. Add Nutritional (Primary) Yeast, 2 tablespoons per meal, to prevent fleas.

3. Add raw garlic in any form (diced or juiced) to their meals, to prevent worms. For garlic juice: Blend 5 cloves of garlic with 2 cups of water.

4. Add 2 tablespoons of oil per day to meals, to aid digestion.

5. Blend any leftover or raw vegetables, and add to grains.

6. Kelp and dulse are good for cats' food, for a fishy taste.

7. Blend fresh wheatgrass and comfrey leaves and add to their meals, to help skin and general health.

8. Add soaked and sprouted legumes, seeds, nuts and grains to diet.

9. Warm food before serving.

CEREAL
2 meals

6 cups water	1 cup rye flakes or wheat flakes
1 cup oats	1/2 cup cracked wheat

In a large pot, combine the water and grains. Cook over medium heat until it begins to bubble. Reduce heat and cook for 20 minutes, until the grains are soft but firm.

VEGETABLE MEDLEY FOR PUPPIES
2 meals

1/2 cup stock or water	2 teaspoons wheat germ
2 carrots, diced	2 tablespoons peanut butter
2 celery stalks, diced	1 teaspoon sweetener
1/2 medium size zucchini, sliced	(sorghum or date sugar)

Put in blender: the stock, diced carrots, and zucchini; blend at medium speed for 1 minute. Add the celery, wheat germ, peanut butter, and sweetener, and blend for 1 minute more. Transfer to a large pot and warm. Add 3 tablespoons of cereal, if desired.

As your dog gets older, increase the amount of cereal.

DRY MIX
or
GRANOLA FOR A HAPPY DOG
4 meals

4 cups oats	1/4 cup sorghum
2 cups wheat flakes or rye flakes	1/3 cup oil
1 cup cracked wheat	1/3 cup water
1/2 cup whole wheat flour	

Preheat oven to 275 F. In a large bowl, combine all the dry ingredients. In a separate bowl, combine all the liquid ingredients; add to the dry and mix thoroughly. Bake for one hour, stirring every 20 minutes to keep in small bits.

Serve in combination with other dinner suggestions.

KASHA AND CEREAL
2 meals

2 cups cooked kasha (buckwheat groats)	3 tablespoons peanut butter
1 cup cooked cereal mixture	1 cup water
(see recipe)	

In a large saucepan, combine kasha and cereal; add the peanut butter and water. Place over medium heat; warm and serve.

LENTIL AND BARLEY LOAF
2 meals

2 cups water
1/2 cup dried lentils, washed
1/3 cup barley

1/3 cup chopped onion
1/2 cup chopped celery
1/2 teaspoon sea salt

In a large pot, bring the water to a boil. Add the lentils and the barley; reduce heat, cover and simmer for 25 minutes, or until barley is tender. Now put the onions and celery in a blender; blend at medium speed for 1 minute, and add to the grains.
Season with salt and garlic powder.

POTATO AND CEREAL DINNER
2 meals

7 potatoes

1 cup cooked cereal (see recipe)

Wash and cube the potatoes. Place in a pot with water to cover, and cook over medium heat for 25 minutes, till soft enough to mash. Mash well and season with 1/8 cup tamari and 1/8 cup tahini, if desired. Add the cereal.

OATMEAL QUICKIE
2 meals

4 cups oats
9 cups water

1/2 teaspoon salt
2 slices whole wheat bread, cubed

Put the oats and water in a large pot. Cook over low heat for 20 minutes, till mixture is creamy. Remove from heat and add remaining ingredients.

OKARA DELIGHT
3 meals

(Okara: soy pulp, by-product of making tofu)

2 cups okara
1 cup cooked millet
2 cups raw vegetables, blended

1 slice whole wheat bread, cubed
2 tablespoons oil
4 cups water or stock

Combine all the ingredients in a large bowl. Serve warm.

VARIATION

Substitute any grain for the millet.

SOYBEAN MASH
1 meal

2 cups cooked soybeans
1 cup tomato juice or stock

1 slice bread, cubed
3 tablespoons oil

Mash the soybeans in a large bowl. Add the remaining ingredients, and mix well.

RICE-MILLET VEGETABLE DISH
2 meals

1 cup cooked rice
1 cup cooked millet
3 cups leftover vegetables

1/4 cup oil
1/2 cup water

Put in a large pot: the rice, millet, oil, and water. Put vegetables in blender and blend at medium speed until creamy; add to the grains. Serve warm.

ANY-KIND BEAN DISH
2 meals

3 cups cooked beans (pinto,
   limas, navy, soy, or kidney)

1/4 cup oil
1 cup cracked wheat

Combine all ingredients in a large bowl; lightly mash.

BREAKFAST SPECIAL
2 meals

5 apples, cubed
2 cups water

4 ripe bananas, mashed
2 cups cooked cereal

Put the apples and water in a blender; blend at medium speed for 30 seconds. Add to the bananas and cereal, and mix well. Add some dry mix (see recipe) if desired.

POTATO SKINS
Serves 2

6 to 8 baked potatoes (leftovers)

Peel skins off leftover potatoes; cut skins into bite-size pieces. Mix with soy meal, grains, and leftover vegetables. Makes a big hit with dogs!

CHICK-PEA STEW
2 meals

3 cups cooked chick-peas
3 tablespoons oil
3 tablespoons peanut butter
2 cups water or stock

1 carrot, diced
1 celery stalk, diced
1/2 onion, chopped
1 beet, diced

Mash the chick-peas in a large bowl. Add the oil, peanut butter, and 1 cup of the water. Put in blender: the remaining water, the carrot, celery, onion, and beet; blend at medium speed for 30 seconds. Add to the chick-peas and serve warm.

BULGHUR DINNER
2 meals

3 cups of bulghur
7 cups of water or stock
2 carrots, diced
1 zucchini, diced

1 green pepper, diced
1 small onion, diced
3 garlic cloves, diced

Soak the bulghur in 6 cups of water. Put 1 cup water and remaining ingredients in a blender; blend at medium speed for 30 seconds.
  Combine both mixtures; warm and serve.

INSTANT SOYBEAN-MEAL DINNER
2 meals

5 cups water or stock
2 cups soybean meal*

1/2 onion blended in 1/2 cup water
1/2 cup cooked rice

Bring the water to a boil, in a large pot over medium heat. Reduce heat; add soybean meal, and cook for 5 minutes. Add the onion and cooked rice, and remove from heat.
  *Soybean meal can be purchased at most grain mills.

KITTY CAT SPECIAL

1 12-ounce cake tofu
1 tablespoon nutritional yeast
1 teaspoon kelp

1 teaspoon chopped dulse
1 tablespoon oil

Mash the tofu and add the remaining ingredients.

(We have found that dogs and cats love avocados. Whenever you can, add cubed avocado pieces to their meals. It is excellent for their coats; lots of unsaturated natural oils, and full of vitamins and minerals.)

AVOCADO-TOFU DINNER

1 8-ounce cake tofu, mashed   1 medium-sized avocado, mashed

Mash together and serve.

STEAMED VEGIES AND AVOCADO
Yields 3 meals

1/2 head cabbage (medium-sized),   2 onions, sliced
  chopped   3 potatoes, cubed
3 carrots, sliced   1 ripe avocado
1 zucchini, sliced

Steam vegetables in large pot, for about 15 to 20 minutes. (Use minimal amount of water, and a steamer rack or basket.)
Mix together the avocado and vegies.

AVOCADO AND SWEET POTATOES
Yields 2 meals

4 sweet potatoes   2 slices bread, pieced
1 avocado, mashed   2 tablespoons nutritional yeast

Steam or bake sweet potatoes. Remove and discard skins. Combine sweet potatoes with all the other ingredients.

Recipes For Dogs And Cats
Index

The Spirit of Ahimsa

Thoughts on dynamic harmlessness,
expressed in daily life as veganism.
By H. Jay Dinshah, President,
The American Vegan Society
Malaga, New Jersey 08328

As I have implied, veganism involves no animal-source foods or products. We do not use animal flesh of course, because of the killing but also because of the terrible cruelties and abnormal conditions involved in all the stages of the life of the animal in captivity, from the moment of conception to the moment of slaughter. I shall not go into these in detail here, as they are well documented in vegetarian and other literature, and are readily seen and learned on the farm, in books, at the slaughterhouse, etc.

But it is less well known that the production of milk requires animals to be artificially bred, fattened, and killed: the innocent calves that are born to keep their mothers in lactation (giving milk), and are destined for a short and sad life before meeting their "destiny" as platefuls of veal. The conditions of raising these calves in modern intensive production, are so pathetic and disgraceful that it is difficult to understand how the mind of man can think of such things to inflict upon helpless creatures— excepting for one factor: the profit involved. This is the key, always the profit motive.

In the dairy industry, as in all phases of animal husbandry, everything must turn a profit or it must "go" (to the slaughter) and the sooner the better. Artificial devices of every possible kind are used to make the mother cow give more and more milk: hormones, overfeeding, over-breeding, this, that, and the other thing; and when her overworked body rebels against it, she is drugged and doped up just as we drug our own bodies (if we live in the conventional manner) into some outer semblance of "health".

Mastitis and even less pleasant diseases are common in the dairy industry; however, a veterinarian (who was himself a vegetarian) once told us that "the slaughterhouse is the farmer's best friend" for disposing of diseased animals—to be used for human food. If thinking about this makes one wish to stop eating meat, it is certainly no recommendation for the use of milk!

Eggs are the furthest thing from a reasonable and wholesome food for humans that it is possible to find. One need only apply the test of Truth to the precise source of the egg, the anatomical relation to the rest of the hen's body, the organs producing the material, and to what manner of waste in the human female it corresponds; and if this test of Truth be objectively applied, the result must be an immediate and final cessation of the use of eggs by such a person making the test. But we do not deal with these facts alone. The compassionate viewpoint that we take for the cow is just as valid in application to the hen....

The vegan protests, with all his heart, mind, and soul, against not only the manner in which the killing is done, not only against the killing itself, but against the whole selfish and ignoble system of breeding, raising, penning, castrating, doping, disrupting of families, enslaving, and of course the final scene in the whole unholy drama: the killing act itself.

The vegan recognizes the impossibility of separating the cruelty and killing from the business of keeping animals, or obtaining animal products, on a sound and profitable basis in a modern competitive society. Thus the vegan resolves to "root out the whole forest" of cruelty and suffering, not merely chop down a single tree!

(Out Of The Jungle, chapter 4)

To tell the truth, we must live it. Only when our every thought, word, and deed can stand the strong light of conscientious scrutiny can we truly be called truthful. Every sincere and earnest seeker comes upon many "Moments Of Truth" in his lifetime; such a test may come at any time, from any quarter; indeed, our very lives seem to be made up of a series of such tests, which if viewed rightly are to be considered as opportunities for further progress and growth. For, how one faces up to such trials of truth is a measure and an exercise of one's real character, virtue, moral fiber, and spiritual progress.

When one's attention has been drawn to injustice, cruelty, exploitation, suffering and pain, does one greet the revelation with a head-in-the-sand attitude? Or does he meet it in the forthright manner, searching his soul to learn what he can do to remedy (not merely alleviate) the situation? We should certainly agree by now that the real way to root out any such wrong-doing is to dig it out by the roots, or dry it up at the source; in short, to eliminate the CAUSE, not just fool around with effects. The wise man looks to causes, realizing that effects will follow naturally.

There are two ways to even act upon the truth, once one has decided to do something about a situation. One way is the half-hearted and half-baked way: pussy-footing around, just doing enough to lull a semi-developed conscience back into blissful slumber. The other way is the way of the man with a well-developed conscience and a realization that principles are not negotiable pawns with which to barter for favor and position in the world.

After all, every man must live with his own conscience. Let fools forsake his company; let relatives sigh over his "eccentricities"; what means this to a man who has made his peace with his inner self? What is the value of fickle friendship or pleasure that is purchased at the cost of principle and self-respect? And what is the value of fashions or creature comforts if produced through the agony of others?

(Here's Harmlessness, chapter 16)

In this modern age of mass communication, a sweeping numbness has developed in many minds, a form of defense mechanism or reaction to the over-stimulation of our senses by visual and auditory gimmicks. We see so much, and hear so much; but so much of what we see and hear just isn't so. So much is just tinsel, tinplate, and trickery. There is so much artificiality and puffery and sham on every hand, that even if the "real thing" comes along, it may well be lost in the shuffle, overwhelmed by the blare of neon, newsprint, and night-life.

The Golden Rule is the "real thing." It gives us at once a firm foundation on which to build a solid structure of ethical living and moral behavior. It immediately sweeps away the cold cynicism of the "what's in it for me?" philosophy; it devastates the "life is a vacuum" theories; it junks the "dog-eat-dog" principle.

(Out Of The Jungle, chapter 1)

Mankind has been in the jungle too long. As with a mole or owl viewing the bright sunshine, we are presently so dazzled by the brilliance of what may lie ahead, that we prefer the comfort of our present position. We are possessed by a great inertia; we cling to that which we think we know, rather than attempting that which we do not yet fully understand. We despise something that might be infinitely better for us, because we do not bother to learn of its benefits.

If we were ever to rid ourselves of the "jungle law" complex with which we so blithely cover our most shameful actions, who knows where the Path might lead us? The world is, after all, much more than just a jungle. We might come out of the darkness into the lovely sunshine, and become used to the bright light after a while. We might follow the Path much further than we can see as yet, hiding as we do behind the twisted vines and weeds of our own distorted world-view.

The Path might lead us through lovely gardens and along beautiful brooksides, through green meadows and by great rivers of real wisdom and thought. We might wend our way up to the pinnacle of a lofty mountain; or, freed from the terrible tangle of our own mental and moral shortcomings (self-imposed, to be sure), we might even find that we can soar in the skies of progress and enlightenment. We will never see the realization of such dreams if we are content to go on living a life in emulation of the hyena, the jackal, and the tiger.

(Out Of The Jungle, chapter 6)

We hold this truth to be self-evident, that all animals are endowed by their Creator with certain inalienable rights; that among these are Life, Liberty, and the Pursuit of Happiness.

THE ANIMAL ANTHEM

GOD blessed His animals
Friends whom we love;
We'll stand beside them
And guide them
Through this night
With a Light
From above.

On the mountains,
On the prairies,
In the forests,
In the sky and in the sea!
GOD blessed His animals
We'll set them free!
GOD BLESSED HIS ANIMALS
WE'LL SET THEM FREE!

"I do not regard flesh-food as necessary for us at any stage and under any clime in which it is possible for human beings ordinarily to live. I hold flesh-food to be unsuited to our species."

"In my opinion there are definite drawbacks in taking milk or meat. In order to get meat we have to kill. And we are certainly not entitled to any other milk except the mother's milk in our infancy. Over and above the moral drawback, there are others, purely from the point of view of health. Both milk and meat bring with them the defects of the animal from which they are derived. Domesticated cattle are hardly ever perfectly healthy. Just like man, cattle suffer from innumerable diseases. Several of these are overlooked even when the cattle are subjected to periodical medical examinations."..

"I abhor vivisection with my whole soul. I detest the unpardonable slaughter of innocent life in the name of science and of humanity so-called, and all the scientific discoveries stained with innocent blood I count as of no consequence."

Mahatma Gandhi

A Beautiful Bouquet Of Bonus Recipes

(New with 2nd or 3rd Edition.)

Breakfast Recipes

LIGHT DELICIOUS PANCAKES
Yields approximately 4 dozen

2 cups whole wheat flour, sifted
3 tablespoons maple syrup
1 teaspoon baking soda, sifted
1/3 cup oil
2-1/2 cups tofu milk
 (1-3/4 cups water, blended with
 8-ounce cake of tofu)
 plus
1-1/2 cups water

*Optional:
1/2 cup fresh blueberries
1/4 cup soaked raisins
1/4 cup grated apple
1/4 cup sliced banana

 *You can add ONE of the optional ingredients to the batter.

Mix all dry ingredients together. Mix liquid ingredients and then pour into the dry mixture. Mix thoroughly but leave some lumps which make the pancakes fluffy; if you smooth it out too much, it makes the pancakes tough. You should be able to pour the batter; if too thick, add a little water.

 Lightly oil skillet or griddle. Make sure griddle or skillet is very hot (to test, a drop of water should bead on skillet). Pour a tablespoonful of batter on skillet. When it starts to bubble, flip and cook 2 to 3 minutes more. Serve with maple syrup or jam.

AMBROSIA
Serves 2

1/4 cup almonds
1/4 cup raisins
1/4 cup prunes, pitted

1/4 cup dried shredded coconut
water

Place ingredients in a jar. Add twice as much water to it as there are nuts and dried fruit. Place in refrigerator overnight. Add to a fruit bowl or granola in the morning.

AVOCADO JUBILEE
Serves 2 to 4

1 ripe avocado, peeled and diced
1 apple, peeled and diced
1 orange, peeled and diced
1 grapefruit, peeled and diced
1 banana, sliced

1/4 cup raisins
3 tablespoons shredded coconut
3 tablespoons wheat germ or bran
1 to 2 cups orange juice

Mix all ingredients in a bowl; chill, and serve.

SWEET NUT CANDIES
Yields 4 loaves or 60 candies

1 cup fresh coconut, shredded
4 cups walnuts, almonds, pecans,
  ground finely
3 cups sunflower seeds, ground
1-1/2 cups rolled oats covered with
  1/4 cup maple syrup
1 cup wheat germ
1 cup soaked raisins,
  half of them chopped
1 cup raisins
2/3 cup tahini

1 banana, ripe
1/2 cup plain rolled oats
1/2 cup maple syrup and
  1/2 cup maple sugar
OR 1 cup sweetener
1-1/2 teaspoons cinnamon
1/3 teaspoon nutmeg
1/8 teaspoon allspice
1 cup nuts or sunflower seeds,
  ground finely (for topping)

In a large bowl, combine the coconut, ground nuts (either one kind or a combination), ground sunflower seeds, oats covered with syrup, and wheat germ. Mix well. Add the soaked raisins (or diced prunes or dates if desired).

In a blender, mix 2/3 cup water (use the raisin water), dry raisins, tahini, and banana. Add this mixture to the above ingredients. Then add the dry oats, maple syrup and maple sugar. You may want to add another 1/4 cup of sweetener. If the mixture is too wet, add more wheat germ or ground sunflower seeds to absorb the moisture. Sprinkle in cinnamon, nutmeg, allspice, and stir well.

Roll the mixture into little candies or balls, or shape into loaves, then roll them around in the chopped nuts. You can decorate the candies with a nut in the middle. Chill for a few hours or overnight to solidify.

Soups and Sandwiches

QUICK SOY CHEESE PIZZA

2 slices of whole wheat bread,
  or open pita bread
1/4 cup tomato sauce
A pinch of oregano

A pinch of garlic powder
1/2 teaspoon oil
1/4 cup grated soy cheese

Coat bread lightly with oil and sprinkle with garlic powder. Then toast bread in a toaster oven, or oven, until lightly browned. Spread with tomato sauce, covering all edges of the bread; sprinkle oregano and grated cheese on top, and lightly drip oil onto the cheese. Place back into toaster oven and bake at 350 F. until cheese is melted—approximately 5 minutes. Voila! Pizza!

For variety, you can add mashed tofu, sliced tofu, sliced tomatoes, onions, mushrooms, or peppers. Try it, you'll love it.

Salads

TAHINI FRUIT SALAD
Serves 2 to 4

Sauce
   1/2 cup tahini
   1/2 cup water or apple juice

   2 tablespoons sorghum

Mix all sauce ingredients together until creamy smooth. Add more water if necessary.

Salad
   2 medium apples, diced
   1/2 cup seedless grapes
   1 peach, diced
   1 pear, diced

   1 ripe banana, sliced
   8 almonds, slivered
   1/2 cup raisins

Place all cut-up fruit into a bowl. Pour sauce over it, stir, and serve.

STUFFED AVOCADO WITH TOFU
Serves 4

   2 large ripe avocados
   1 small onion, peeled and diced
   1 medium tomato, diced
   1 sweet red pepper, diced
   1/2 cup fresh mushrooms, diced
   1 stalk celery, diced

   3 tablespoons tamari
   2 tablespoons nutritional yeast
   1 cup mashed tofu
   1 tablespoon apple cider vinegar
      (optional)

Cut avocados in half. Scoop out all the avocado, mash and mix with remaining ingredients. Put mixture back into the avocado shells, and serve at room temperature.

Side Dishes

Beginner Recipes

SAUCEY BAKED ONIONS
Yields 1 medium-sized casserole

5 to 7 medium onions,
   peeled and quartered

1 cup tahini dressing (see recipe)
2 to 3 tablespoons nutritional yeast

Place quartered onions in a baking dish. Mix in tahini dressing and nutritional yeast. Bake 30 to 40 minutes at 350 F.

FRIED SHREDDED CARROT
Serves 2

2 tablespoons oil
2 garlic cloves, diced
4 carrots, shredded
2 tablespoons tamari

4 tablespoons nutritional yeast
1/4 teaspoon fresh ginger, minced
   (optional)

Heat the oil in a skillet over medium heat. Saute garlic for 1 minute. Stir in carrots and remaining ingredients. Stir-fry for a few minutes, until carrots are tender.

MARINATED TOFU
Serves 4 to 6

2 lbs. tofu, cut into big chunks
1/3 cup stock or water
1/4 cup nutritional yeast
1/4 cup tahini

1/4 cup tamari
2 tablespoons apple cider vinegar
1/4 teaspoon garlic powder
1/4 teaspoon ginger powder

Blend all ingredients except tofu. Marinate the tofu in the mixture for several hours. Drain off liquid. Chill and serve, OR, heat 2 tablespoons of oil in a medium skillet and stir-fry for 5 minutes, OR, bake marinated tofu with remaining liquid on an oiled baking sheet for 1/2 hour at 325 F.
   Great served on top of noodles.

Main Dishes

SPAGHETTI AND TOFU
Serves 2

1 cup tofu, mashed
2 tablespoons nutritional yeast
1 tablespoon oil
2 tablespoons tamari

2 cups spaghetti, cooked
3 cups tomato sauce,
  or any favorite sauce

In a medium-sized bowl, mix the tofu, nutritional yeast, oil, and tamari. Stir in the spaghetti and sauce. Heat and serve.

BAKED MACARONI AND TOFU
Serves 3 to 4

4 cups macaroni, cooked
1 cup tofu, mashed

3 cups cheesy gravy (see recipe)

Preheat oven to 350 F. Combine tofu and macaroni. Place in a baking dish. Pour gravy over mixture, and bake for 20 minutes.

COLD KASHA BURGERS
Yields 2-1/2 dozen

3 cups kasha
2 onions, diced
2 stalks celery, diced
3 carrots, diced or grated
3 to 4 tablespoons tahini

2 tablespoons oil
1/4 cup tamari,
  or seasoning, or sea salt
2 tablespoons nutritional yeast

Bring 6 cups of water to boil in large pot. Add kasha and cook over medium-low heat for 10 minutes, or until soft. Vegies may be raw or lightly sauteed.

Add remaining ingredients and mix well. Form mixture into patties and place on a tray. Serve or chill.

VARIATION

Use bulghur instead of kasha. You can simply soak the bulghur for 1 hour instead of cooking, if you desire a chewier texture.

RAW SUNNYBURGERS
Yields 40 small burgers

4-1/2 to 5-1/2 cups
    sunflower seeds
5 carrots, grated finely
2 beets, grated finely
2 stalks celery, diced
1 medium zucchini, diced
    (optional)

2 onions, diced
3 tablespoons tamari
3 tablespoons tahini
1/2 cup nutritional yeast
1/4 cup wheat germ (optional)
1/4 cup sesame seeds (optional)

Blend most of the sunflower seeds dry in a blender, until finely powdered. Leave some whole for crunchiness. Mix with vegetables. Add tamari to taste, and any favorite seasonings. Add nutritional yeast so mixture is not too wet. You can add sesame seeds or wheat germ to help consistency.

    Add tahini; mix well. Shape into small patties, and place on a tray. Serve, or refrigerate for 1/2 hour.

    Serving suggestion: Top with your favorite sauce.

VARIATION

Preheat oven to 350 F. Oil a cookie sheet. Place patties on sheet and bake 15 minutes on one side; then turn over and bake 15 minutes on other side.

TOFU OMELETTE
Serves 1 to 2

1 8-ounce cake tofu
3 tablespoons nutritional yeast
1 tablespoon tamari

2 tablespoons oil
1/4 teaspoon turmeric

Mash the tofu in a bowl. Mix in remaining ingredients. Lightly oil skillet. Place on medium heat. Place batter in skillet and press into omelette shape. Fry until brown on one side, then flip over and brown on other side.

VARIATION

1 onion, diced finely

1/2 sweet red pepper, diced finely

Saute onion and pepper first. Add to batter before frying.

TOFU CUTLETS
Serves 4

2 8-ounce cakes tofu
2 tablespoons tamari
1 cup nutritional yeast
1/2 teaspoon oil

1/4 teaspoon basil
1/4 teaspoon oregano
1 large onion, diced
2 cloves garlic, diced

Drain tofu well of its water. Cut tofu into slices 1/4'' thick. Saute onions and garlic until golden brown. Make a mixture of tamari, oil, saute, and spices. Add other favorite spices if you like.

Place tofu pieces in mixture and let marinate, then dip into nutritional yeast until thoroughly covered.

Oil a cookie sheet. Place tofu pieces on sheet and bake at 325 F. for 5 to 7 minutes on each side, then broil until crispy. This dish can also be cooked in a frying pan with a little oil. Easy and delicious.

VARIATION

Add 2 tablespoons of lemon juice to marinate mixture.

TOFU LOAF
Serves 4 to 6

1 tablespoon oil
2 garlic cloves, diced
1 onion, diced
1 carrot, diced
1 red pepper, diced
1 celery stick, diced
2 tablespoons tamari
2 lbs. tofu, mashed
4 slices whole wheat bread

1 tablespoon oil
1 tablespoon tamari
1/2 teaspoon garlic powder
1 cup nutritional yeast
1/2 cup tahini or peanut butter
1/2 teaspoon basil
1/2 teaspoon oregano
1/2 teaspoon turmeric

Heat 1 tablespoon of oil in a medium skillet; add garlic, onion, pepper, carrot, and celery. Season with 1 tablespoon tamari. When vegetables are tender, remove from heat and put in medium bowl, add mashed tofu. Cut bread into small crouton-sized pieces; quick fry in 1 tablespoon oil, 1 tablespoon tamari, 1/2 teaspoon garlic powder, and 5 tablespoons nutritional yeast. Add bread to tofu mixture, and season with remaining ingredients. Combine well. Place batter into a well oiled casserole; bake at 350 F. for 35 minutes.

Allow to cool; slide a butter knife along the sides, then turn upside-down on a plate to remove from casserole.

Tastes great served with a sauce topping, or, can be used to make sandwiches.

Treats and Beverages

NEW CAROB CAKE
Yields 2 cakes

3 cups whole wheat flour, sifted
1-1/2 teaspoons baking soda
1/2 teaspoon sea salt
3/4 cup carob powder, sifted
3/4 cup oil

2 cups sweetener (maple syrup, sorghum, date sugar, or a combination of all three)
2 teaspoons vanilla
2 cups tofu milk

In a medium bowl, mix together flour, baking soda, sea salt, and carob powder. In a separate bowl, blend together oil, sweetener and vanilla. To make tofu milk, place 1-1/3 cups of water in blender with 8 ounces of tofu—blend until smooth. Slowly add the sweet liquid mixture and milk (alternately) to the flour mixture.

Oil the cake pans. Pour the batter in, filling half-way. Bake at 350 F. for 40-45 minutes, until a toothpick comes out clean.

PEACH PIE A LA RAW
Yields 1 pie

Crust
1-1/2 cups sesame seeds
   and/or sunflower seeds
   blended finely in blender
1/2 cup walnuts and/or almonds
   blended finely

2 tablespoons oil
1 tablespoons raisins,
   blended with
1 to 2 tablespoons fruit juice

In a medium-sized mixing bowl, combine seeds and nuts with the oil. Add the blended raisins. Form into a soft dough. If too wet, add more blended seeds and nuts. Press into a 9-inch pie pan.

Filling
20 peaches, peeled,
   cut and cored
1/2 teaspoon cinnamon

1/4 cup nuts, chopped
1/2 cup raisins

Mix all the ingredients in a large bowl. Place in the pie shell and chill.

VARIATIONS

Filling
   Add 2 mashed bananas in with the peaches.
   Add sliced bananas on top of pie, and sprinkle with shredded coconut.

CAROB PUDDING VARIATION
Yields 4 to 6 cups

Nut milk
2-2/3 cups water
1/2 of 8-ounce cake tofu

1/3 cup tahini
1/2 cup peanut butter

Put nut milk ingredients together in blender and blend well.

Pudding
1/2 cup sorghum, or
  1/4 cup sorghum and
  1/4 cup date sugar
1/3 cup carob powder

6 tablespoons arrowroot powder
1 teaspoon vanilla
1 teaspoon Postum

Combine nut milk with pudding ingredients, in blender; blend at high speed for 1 minute. Put mixture in a large saucepan; cook over low heat, stirring constantly, for 7 to 10 minutes, till thick. Transfer to cups and chill.

CARROT CAKE
Yields 2 cakes

3/4 cup safflower oil
1-3/4 to 2 cups sweetener
  (date sugar or sorghum)
1 cup thick tahini milk
  (see recipe)
4 cups whole wheat flour
1-1/2 teaspoons baking soda

2 teaspoons cinnamon
1/2 teaspoon allspice
2-1/2 cups carrots, grated
1 cup soaked raisins, drained
  (optional)
1/2 cup nuts, chopped (optional)

In a large bowl, combine oil, sweetener, and tahini milk. Stir well. Add grated carrots, raisins, and nuts to the liquid mixture.

In a separate bowl, mix flour, baking soda, cinnamon, and allspice. Add dry mixture to liquid slowly, stirring constantly.

Preheat oven to 350 F. Bake 40 to 50 minutes in oiled baking dish.

SPICE COOKIES
Yields 3 dozen

3/4 cup oil
1-1/2 cups sweetener
4 tablespoons tahini, mixed with
  8 tablespoons water
3 teaspoons vanilla
4 cups whole wheat pastry flour

1 teaspoon baking soda
3 teaspoons cinnamon
1/4 teaspoon allspice
1 cup soaked raisins, drained
  (optional)

In a large bowl, combine the oil, sweetener, tahini/water mixture; add the vanilla and mix well. Stir raisins in.

In a separate bowl, combine the flour and spices; and baking soda, raisins, and nuts.

Mix the dry mixture into the liquid batter, stirring until a smooth consistency.

The batter should be fairly dry. Roll batter into small balls, and press down lightly onto an oiled cookie sheet.

Preheat oven at 350 F. Bake 8 to 10 minutes.

BANANA TAHINI TIDBITS
Serves 2 to 4

2 frozen bananas, sliced
2 to 3 tablespoons tahini

1 tablespoon sorghum
1 to 2 tablespoons water

Mix tahini, sorghum and water together. Place sliced bananas on a plate. Spread tahini mixture on them. Place in the freezer until mixture freezes; then serve, or keep in freezer as a frozen treat for any time of the day.

SLIPPERY ELM TAHINI DRINK
Yields 3 cups

2-1/2 cups boiling water
2 teaspoons slippery elm powder
2 teaspoons tahini

1 teaspoon vanilla
1 to 2 teaspoons sweetener

Blend for 30 seconds, and serve warm.

TAHINI MILK
Yields 1-1/2 cups

1 cup water, ice cold
1/4 cup tahini

1/2 teaspoon vanilla (optional)
1 teaspoon sweetener (optional)

Blend well in blender. Good in baking recipes.

ALMOND MILK
Yields 1 quart

1 quart water, ice cold
1/2 to 1 cup soaked almonds

2 tablespoons raisins, or
1 tablespoon sweetener

Put all ingredients in blender, and blend at high speed for 2 minutes. Serve over granola or cereal.

SUNNY MILK
Yields 1 quart plus

1 quart water, ice cold
1/2 to 1 cup sunflower seeds
1/2 ripe banana (optional)

1 tablespoon sorghum, or
3 tablespoons raisins

Put all ingredients in blender, and blend at high speed for 2 minutes. Serve as a drink or over granola. Add banana for a thicker milk.
  Excellent on breakfast cereal.

VARIATION

Soak seeds overnight, then blend.

NATURAL REMEDIES AND HERBS

We have found some herbs to work better than others. Here is a list of herbs and other natural healing remedies which have worked in treating ourselves.

ALOE— A cactus-type plant. The inside is jelly-like and excellent for burns of any type. Apply the jelly directly to the skin; it is very soothing, gives fast relief, and helps healing.

AVOCADO FACIAL— The oils from this fruit are excellent for the skin. Apply a small amount of mashed avocado to the face, and wash off after 5 minutes. Leaves skin soft.

CAYENNE AND ORANGE JUICE— A drink made of 1 cup warm orange juice and 1/8 teaspoon cayenne. Good for colds; breaks up mucus.

CLAY AND WHEATGRASS— Good for skin irritations. Blend a handful of wheatgrass with 1/4 cup of water. Mix this liquid with herbal clay —enough to make a paste. It's also good for insect bites or stings.

EYEBRIGHT— Make a mild tea for eyewash.

GARLIC— Good for colds and sore throats. Peel and dice fine, then swallow; or suck on a whole peeled clove.

GOLDEN SEAL POWDER— Apply to cuts as a paste or powder to stop bleeding. Good on skin rashes. Taken internally to cleanse body.

GOLDEN SEAL POWDER AND MYRRH— A tea made from this is a good mouth rinse for sensitive or sore gums.

NETTLE TEA— Good for hair rinse; treats dandruff and dryness.

ORANGE— For hiccups, suck on a quarter of an orange.

PEPPERMINT TEA— Good for upset stomach and indigestion.

POTATO POULTICE— Aids in drawing out poisons. Grate a small portion of a peeled potato; apply to infection.

RED CLOVER TEA— Helps clear up skin rashes when taken internally or applied externally.

SENNA TEA— Good as a laxative.

SLIPPERY ELM POWDER— The inner bark from an elm tree. Good for soothing and coating upset stomachs. Can also be used as a thickening agent in cooking. Good in ice cream, hot drinks, and whips. Also gives an added touch to smoothies.

WHEAT GERM OIL— Good as a linament for dry skin. Also good for skin burns.

WINTERGREEN— Good for sore muscles and strains.

In Vegan Cuisine

"WHERE THE PROTEIN IS"

Protein resides in abundance in the following food groups. Remember that creating meals that COMBINE foods from several different groups increases the value of the protein.

WHOLE GRAINS: Cereals, breads, pastas, or "dinner" grains like rice, millet, barley, corn, etc., in millet casseroles, grain loaves, sauteed vegetables over rice, whole grain noodles in lasagna, spaghetti, etc.

LEGUMES: The entire bean family, including versatile soybean products like tofu and texturized vegetable protein (t.v.p.), in e.g. tofu sandwich spreads or cutlets, tofu omelets, tofu or t.v.p. mixed into spaghetti sauce or vegetable and grain casseroles, tofu puddings and desserts; peas; all sprouts (alfalfa, soy, mung, lentil, chick pea, sunflower seed, etc.) served raw in salads; lentils, and garbanzo beans, cooked or made into spreads like "hummus".

GREEN VEGETABLES: Broccoli, spinach, collards, beet tops, kale, mustard greens—lightly steamed, or served raw in salads or with dips—are excellent protein sources.

SEEDS AND NUTS: Sunflower seeds, pumpkin seeds, sesame seeds (tahini—see Glossary), peanuts, almonds, walnuts, cashews, filberts, brazils, macademias, pistachios; in salads, dinner meals like sautes; nut butters on whole grain bread for sandwiches; with breakfast cereals, fruit bowls, desserts, etc.

"WHERE THE MINERALS ARE"

CALCIUM:
Green leafy vegetables: kale, broccoli, collards (1 cup of any of these greens, cooked, has approximately the same calcium content as a 6-oz. glass of milk, with no troublesome phosphate load).

SELENIUM:
Nutritional yeast, broccoli, cabbage, wheat germ, whole grains

IRON:
Molasses/sorghum, dark green leafy vegetables, whole grains, legumes, wheat germ, beets, barley, artichokes, beans, grains, dried apricots.

ZINC:
Nutritional yeast, onions, mushrooms, spinach, soybeans, wheat germ, sunflower seeds, whole grains (sprouted).

"WHERE THE VITAMINS ARE"

For healthy cell metabolism, blood, nerve and muscle function, your body needs two "families" of vitamins, those that dissolve in water, and those that dissolve in oil ("fat-soluble").

1. WATER-SOLUBLE VITAMINS are not stored in the body and must be supplied daily. They are:

"B-COMPLEX" VITAMINS

B-1 (Thiamine)	Choline
B-2 (Riboflavin)	Folic Acid
B-6 (Pyridoxine)	Niacin
Biotin	Other "B-Complex" vitamins

(But see special note on B-12)

A plentiful supply of the B vitamins will be obtained by daily use of a good variety from all these food types: Green and Leafy Vegetables, Whole Grains, Legumes, Nutritional Yeast.

Vitamin C is found in Green and Leafy Vegetables; Fruits such as: Melons, Citrus (Oranges, Grapefruit, Lemons), Tomatoes, Berries.

GREEN VEGETABLES

Alfalfa Sprouts	Collards	Romaine Lettuce
Asparagus	Endive	Spinach
Beans (green)	Kale	Sprouts
Broccoli	Leaf Lettuce	(Mung bean, etc.)
Bok Choy	Leeks	Swiss Chard
Brussels Sprouts	Mustard Greens	Turnip Greens
Cabbage Family	Parsley	etc.

2. FAT-SOLUBLE VITAMINS are stored in the body (notably in the liver), and are needed in the diet 3 to 5 times a week.

Vitamin A is made in the body from provitamin A abundantly supplied by yellow vegetables, especially Carrots, as well as Corn, Pumpkin, Sweet Potato, Rutabaga, and Squash: Acorn, Butternut, Hubbard, Spaghetti, Summer, etc. Yellow Fruits such as Apricots, Peaches, and Tomatoes contain generous amounts, and—perhaps surprisingly—Green Leafy Vegetables (see above listing) are some of the richest sources of provitamin A.

Vitamin E (and Essential Fatty Acids) are in Nuts and Seeds (Almonds, Peanuts, Sunflower Seeds, Sesame Seeds, etc.), and Whole Grains, and their Oils (Corn Oil, Linseed Oil, Safflower Oil, etc.)

Vitamin K is obtained through eating Green Leafy Vegetables.

The following menu guide will help you plan your daily meals. Learn to make one or two dishes for breakfast (cereal, scrambled tofu, etc.), for lunch (soup, salad, sandwiches), and for dinner (grain loaves, vegetable sautés, pastas with sauces, steamed green and yellow vegetables). Use fruits, and baked goods for treats and desserts. Excellent recipes for these and many other dishes are in the chapters of this book.

Start adding these foods to your daily eating and begin to have "vegan days" of completely animal-free meals. After several such days your body will begin to feel lighter and cleaner, you will start to develop favorite dishes and taste treats to look forward to, and you will know that this is the style of eating that will bring you balanced health for a much longer lifetime.

VITAMIN B-12 NOTE: Much unnecessary worry has been generated over "getting enough B-12". Vegans, who probably need less B-12 than omnivores, seldom, if ever, show signs of B-12 deficiency. They obtain their B-12 supplies on the surface of fresh vegetables, in B-12 enriched or fortified foods such as nutritional yeast, soymilk and cereals, and probably B-12 producing bacteria that live in their own mouths and intestines.

Unlike other B vitamins, B-12 is stored in the body for long periods of time. However, because Vitamin B-12 deficiency (though unlikely with balanced vegan nutrition) can be severe, vegans who do not use any of the above B-12 containing foods, should take supplements of B-12 occasionally. One 25 microgram tablet taken weekly, or crushing a few tablets and adding the powder to gravies, soy milks, salad dressings, etc., will make B-12 supplementation convenient for an individual or the whole family. Obtaining sufficient Vitamin B-12 should never be a rationale for eating meat, dairy, or other harmful and unnecessary animal products.

SUGGESTED VEGAN MENU

BREAKFAST

Hot Weather

Cold cereal with nut-milk, sunflower milk, soy milk, fruit, wheat germ, bran.

Whole grain toast and peanut butter or tofu cream cheese spread.

OR

Fruit bowl: melon, avocado, banana, peaches, apples, plums, with sunflower seeds, raisins; topped with tofu yogurt.

OR

Granola with dried fruit, fresh fruit, topped with apple sauce or fruit smoothie.

Cold Weather

Hot grain cereal (millet, oats, cous cous, bulghur) with soy or sunflower milk, fruit, wheat germ, soy margarine.

Hot or Cold Weather

Scrambled tofu "omelet" with whole grain toast, fruit spread, peanut butter, tahini.

Beverages

Hot: Hot carob, Postum, herbal teas, etc.

Cold: Fruit juices, nut milk, smoothies, vegetable juices.

LUNCH

Salads

Tossed Garden
Spinach Mushroom
Sprouts
Guacamole-Avocado
Raw Carrot Salad
Tofu Eggless
Cole Slaw
Potato Salad
Bulghur Tabouli
Hummus (chick peas)
Cold String Bean

Sandwiches

Pizza Sandwich
Whole grain bread with peanut butter, raisins, banana
Tofu Spread
Hummus
Avocado
Grain and vegetable burgers topped with lettuce, tomatoes, onions, avocado, sprouts.

Cold Soup

Gazpacho (tangy vegetable soup)

Hot Soups

Onion
Tomato
Vegetable
Split Pea
Barley
Lentil
Miso

Other suggestions:

Raw vegetables with tahini dip.
Baked beans with corn bread.
Tofu cutlets

DINNER

Salads

See lunch salads

Entrees

Vegetable or super burgers (tofu, sauteed vegetables, and grains of choice)
Vegetable Bake (vegetables, with tahini dressing, tomato sauce, or nutritional yeast gravy)
Stuffed Cabbage
String-bean Soy-cheese Bake
Millet Loaf
Noodles and Tofu
Potato Kugel
Eggplant Milanese
Fried Rice
Potatoes Au Gratin
Vegetable Stir-fry

Treats

Frozen Banana Ice-Cream
Apple Pie
Tofu Cream Pie
Danish
Banana Bread
Carob Pudding
Carob Candy

Snacks

Fruits of all kinds
Crackers and peanut-butter
Fudgesicles
Rich nut "ice cream"
Fruit smoothies
Banana Tahini "Malted"
Cookies:
  Carob
  Peanut Butter
  Oatmeal
  Spice
  Vanilla
Carob Cake

Recipe Index

TIME FOR A NEW WORLD

Time for a new world!

We're waking up to a brighter dream.

Time for a new world!

The morning wakes with a new world theme.

And it sings of a life

That is gentle and high;

Of a day that shall rise

With the sun in the sky.

Time for a new world!

Where Love lifts us,

So we can see the Light.

Time for a new world!

A world in which

Everything is right.

If enough people cared,

We all would be free.

From a dream that is shared,

Comes Reality.

Time for a new world!

Light